Guiding Girls Toward GREATNESS

15 Pillar-Based Lessons To Empower Girls In Grades 5-12

By Melanie Martin

Guiding Girls Toward Greatness: 15 Pillar-Based Lessons To Empower Girls In Grades 5-12

Paperback ISBN: 978-1-57543-255-7
eBook ISBN: 978-1-57543-254-0

Published by Mar*co Products, Inc.
1443 Old York Road
Warminster, PA 18974
1-800-448-2197
www.marcoproducts.com

Cover and text graphic images © Shutterstock.com

MAR*CO

Mar*co Products, Inc.
1443 Old York Road
Warminster, PA 18974
Phone: (215) 956-0313
Fax: (215) 956-9041
http://www.marcoproducts.com

To purchase additional copies of this book or request a catalog, call our customer service department at 1-800-448-2197.

Dedication

I owe a debt of gratitude for the overwhelming support and encouragement of many very special people:

- Lynne E. Muller, Ph.D., former coordinator of school counseling, Baltimore County Public Schools.

- Rowland Savage and Timothy Hayden, my supervisors, for continued mentoring and assistance. Thank you for inspiring school counselors to grow professionally for the betterment of children everywhere.

- The Maryland School Counselors Association and the Baltimore County Association for Counseling and Development for serving as advocates for the school counseling profession and for allowing me to serve among you and work with some of the finest counselors in the field.

- The administration and staff of Hillcrest Elementary School, Windsor Mill Middle School, and Randallstown Elementary School for allowing me the privilege of working with your children.

- United Way of Central Maryland and Procter & Gamble for having a vision and making an investment in the future of young female leaders.

- The hundreds of students who have participated in the Hillcrest Leadership Group and the *Beautiful Divine Ladies* and the *Dream and Flourish* programs and their parents and families for allowing me the privilege of being part of your daughters' growth and development.

- My family, especially my parents Ryland & Diane, my first and best teachers. Thank you for having faith in me; being cheerleaders, worker elves, seamstress, and carpenter; and supporting every project I've ever undertaken. Thank you for imparting to me the life lessons that I hope to share with others.

- To my children Nysa and Isaiah, for being my center and for teaching me something each day about parenting, priorities, patience, prayer, and the purest kind of love. My heart finds a reason to love you just a little bit more every single day.

- And, lastly, my husband Phillip. There has never been a goal I've set for myself that you didn't think I could reach. There has never been an obstacle I've faced that you didn't think I could overcome. Your unwavering belief in me inspires me to try things I never thought I could do. Thank you for being my anchor, my compass, and my best friend. I love you with all my heart.

Contents

Instructions For Using The CD

ADOBE® PDF files of each of the reproducible* pages are included for your use on the CD. Many of these pages are provided in color, but may be printed in either color or grayscale. These files cannot be modified/edited. The files are named to correspond to the pages in the book. For example:

15_GuidingGirls.pdf is the same as page 15 in the book

System requirements to open PDF (.pdf) files: Adobe Reader® 5.0 or newer (compatible with Windows 2000® or newer or Mac OS 9.0® or newer).

***PERMISSION TO REPRODUCE:** The purchaser may reproduce the activity pages, handouts, and forms free and without special permission, for participant use for a particular group or class. Reproduction of these materials for colleagues, an entire school or school system, or for commercial sale is strictly prohibited.

Introduction

Why A Girls Leadership & Empowerment Program?

I like to describe school counselors as being like candle wax, which is strong and substantial before the candle is lit. At the beginning of the school year, counselors build a strong, solid foundation that includes individual and group counseling, classroom lessons, and school-wide programs. All of that is in place, if only in the mind of the counselor, before the first student walks through the first freshly cleaned and buffed hallway. Then the candle is lit and, as the fire grows, the wax melts, moves, and becomes fluid. The same is true of counselors. As emergencies, crises, individual student needs, and changing school climate spark the fire of real life, that strong school counseling program plan changes shape to meet the unique needs of that year's students. That fluidity is what I like best about school counseling: the profession's innate ability to evolve from school year to school year, day to day, even minute by minute to meet each student's needs. What a wonderfully strong and yet adaptable candle is the school counselor!

During my career as an elementary and secondary school counselor, I often found myself assessing female students' needs. I frequently received referrals from girls who were unhappy with their appearance and exhibited low self-esteem, who had difficulty maintaining positive friendships and appropriate peer interactions, or who struggled with breaking away from a negative crowd in order to make positive decisions for themselves. I observed that as they grew into young women, there was a need for special programs and offerings to address these issues. Desiring to be proactive, I began creating guidance lessons related to these topics and designed specifically for female students. Over the years, the lessons evolved into a program to help girls develop leadership skills, build self-esteem, and create a sense of community among their classmates. As members of the program met regularly to learn about such topics as making a positive first impression, developing academic goals, and conflict resolution, an amazing thing happened. The more topics the program covered, the more the girls wanted to learn. The more young women allowed to participate in the program, the more young women applied to participate the next year. The larger the program grew, the more support we received from staff members, parents, and the community.

Our school's program for girls was making a difference that everyone could see. Office referrals declined and students who participated in the program became more successful academically. Our organized initiatives provided our school with a proactive alternative to punitive responses to misbehavior. During the 2005–2006 school year, 48% of public schools took serious disciplinary action against a student. Among these actions, 74% were suspensions lasting five days or more, 5% were expulsions, and 20% were transfers to specialized schools.[1] Our results demonstrated that an alternative to zero-tolerance policies in schools can have "significant positive impacts on student behaviors, as well as on academic achievement."[2] Additionally, the more years a young woman participated in our program, the less likely she was to have disciplinary problems or to be at risk academically. Students also demonstrated a greater investment in themselves and their educational experience. Nationally normed research indicates that participating in after-school programs that promote social skills improves such self-perceptions as self-esteem and self-confidence, and school bonding indicated by participants' attitudes toward school."[3] Social-emotional learning programs have yielded statistically significant improvements in attitude, behaviors, and academic performance.[4] Social and character development programs have had a substantive impact on student altruistic behavior, support for teachers, and feelings of safety.[5] We achieved measurable and immeasurable goals. I think about the student who entered our program as a 6th-grader too timid to speak in public or lift her head to talk to other students and who, in an end-of-year speech, shared advice for new middle school students. I think about the student suspended for fighting and insubordination during the first week of school who, through mentoring and motivation, became a leader and role model. I think about girls who have informed me that they avoided getting into a fight or skipping school because they did not want to lose the opportunity to participate in this program. So as great school counselors everywhere melt like wax to meet the needs of their changing student populations, think about the differences, both large and small, that girls programming can make in the life of developing young women every day, and about what can happen when such programming is needed but is not available.

How To Tell Your School Needs A Program Specifically For Girls

You may have noticed signs that your school's female students need a program tailored just for them. Or you may be wondering how to tell if your school needs such a program. If you're addressing some of the following issues in your student body, this program may be right for your school:

- Helping girls learn to form and maintain positive friendships
- Addressing negative girl groups that form at lunchtime or at recess
- Changing the climate of a grade level with negative girl ringleaders
- Bullying, cyber-bullying, or harassment
- Addressing rumors and name-calling among female students
- Counseling girls who have poor body images or low self-esteem
- Teaching such leadership skills as public speaking or career exploration
- Helping students respond positively to peer pressure

The Elements Of The *Guiding Girls Toward Greatness* Program

The *Guiding Girls Toward Greatness* program is based around the concept of a house, which must have a strong foundation. As you help girls grow and develop into young women, you must also assist them in building a strong foundation. Each lesson in this program contributes to one of the three pillars of the *Guiding Girls Toward Greatness* program:

SELF-ESTEEM BUILDING:

learning to define yourself in positive terms instead of allowing others to define you

LEADERSHIP SKILLS:

learning to make good decisions instead of following a crowd

COMMUNITY BUILDING:

learning to work with others toward positive goals

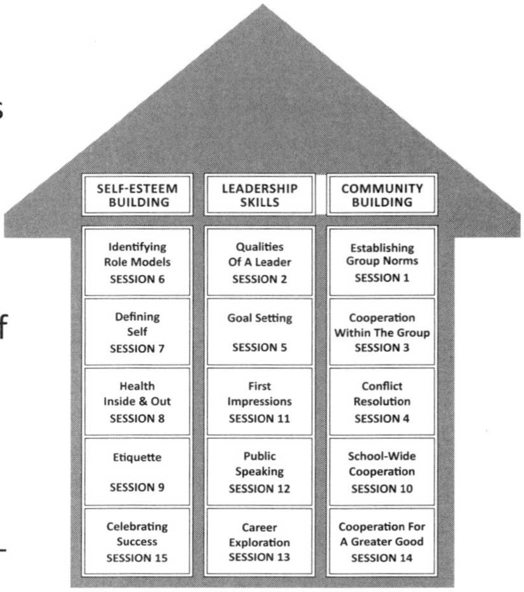

CHOOSING INDIVIDUAL LESSONS:

Use *Sections Organized by Pillar* (page 15) to select individual lessons to meet your needs. Each lesson may be completed with a small counseling group or as a classroom guidance lesson. Many lessons include ideas for extension or inspirational quotations, songs, or concepts to facilitate continued discussion of specific topics.

USING THE ENTIRE PROGRAM AS A CURRICULUM:

This program may be used with young women from individual classes or a specific grade level or as a school-wide program. To utilize this book as a curriculum, present the lessons in sequence. Start by providing each participant with a program folder or binder in which to keep completed activity sheets. This will help students reflect on what they have learned throughout the program and build on previous lessons.

ASCA National Standards Covered Through The *Guiding Girls Toward Greatness* Curriculum

ACADEMIC DEVELOPMENT	
Standard A: Students will acquire the attitudes, knowledge and skills that contribute to effective learning in school and across the life span.	
A:A1	**Improve Academic Self-concept**
A:A1.1	Articulate feelings of competence and confidence as learners
A:A1.2	Display a positive interest in learning
A:A1.3	Take pride in work and achievement
A:A1.5	Identify attitudes and behaviors that lead to successful learning
A:A2	**Acquire Skills For Improving Learning**
A:A2.2	Demonstrate how effort and persistence positively affect learning
A:A3	**Achieve School Success**
A:A3.1	Take responsibility for their actions
A:A3.2	Demonstrate the ability to work independently, as well as the ability to work cooperatively with other students
A:A3.3	Develop a broad range of interests and abilities
A:A3.5	Share knowledge
Standard B: students will complete school with the academic preparation essential to choose from a wide range of substantial post-secondary options, including college.	
A:B1	**Improve Learning**
A:B1.1	Demonstrate the motivation to achieve individual potential
A:B1.2	Learn and apply critical-thinking skills
A:B1.4	Seek information and support from faculty, staff, family and peers
A:B1.5	Organize and apply academic information from a variety of sources
A:B1.7	Become a self-directed and independent learner
A:B2	**Plan to Achieve Goals**
A:B2.1	Establish challenging academic goals in elementary, middle/jr. high and high school
A:B2.2	Use assessment results in educational planning
A:B2.4	Apply knowledge of aptitudes and interests to goal setting
A:B2.5	Use problem-solving and decision-making skills to assess progress toward educational goals
A:B2.7	Identify post-secondary options consistent with interests, achievement, aptitude and abilities
Standard C: students will understand the relationship of academics to the world of work and to life at home and in the community.	
A:C1	**Relate School to Life Experiences**
A:C1.1	Demonstrate the ability to balance school, studies, extracurricular activities, leisure time and life
A:C1.2	Seek co-curricular and community experiences to enhance the school experience
A:C1.3	Understand the relationship between learning and work
A:C1.6	Understand how school success and academic achievement enhance future career and vocational opportunities

CAREER DEVELOPMENT	
Standard A: Students will acquire the skills to investigate the world of work in relation to knowledge of self and to make informed career decisions.	
C:A1	**Develop Career Awareness**
C:A1.1	Develop skills to locate, evaluate and interpret career information
C:A1.2	Learn about the variety of traditional and nontraditional occupations
C:A1.3	Develop an awareness of personal abilities, skills, interests and motivations
C:A1.4	Learn how to interact and work cooperatively in teams
C:A1.5	Learn to make decisions
C:A1.6	Learn how to set goals
C:A1.7	Understand the importance of planning
C:A1.8	Pursue and develop competency in areas of interest
C:A2	**Develop Employment Readiness**
C:A2.7	Develop a positive attitude toward work and learning
C:A2.9	Utilize time- and task-management skills

CAREER DEVELOPMENT	
Standard B: Students will employ strategies to achieve future career goals with success and satisfaction.	
C:B1	**Acquire Career Information**
C:B1.3	Demonstrate knowledge of the career-planning process
C:B1.6	Learn to use the Internet to access career-planning information
C:B2	**Identify Career Goals**
C:B2.1	Demonstrate awareness of the education and training needed to achieve career goals
C:B2.2	Assess and modify their educational plan to support career
Standard C: Students will understand the relationship between personal qualities, education, training and the world of work.	
C:C1	**Acquire Knowledge to Achieve Career Goals**
C:C1.3	Identify personal preferences and interests influencing career choice and success
C:C2	**Apply Skills to Achieve Career Goals**
C:C2.2	Learn how to use conflict management skills with peers and adults
C:C2.3	Learn to work cooperatively with others as a team member

PERSONAL/SOCIAL DEVELOPMENT	
Standard A: Students will acquire the knowledge, attitudes and interpersonal skills to help them understand and respect self and others.	
PS:A1	**Acquire Self-Knowledge**
PS:A1.1	Develop positive attitudes toward self as a unique and worthy person
PS:A1.2	Identify values, attitudes and beliefs
PS:A1.3	Learn the goal-setting process
PS:A1.4	Understand change is a part of growth
PS:A1.5	Identify and express feelings
PS:A1.6	Distinguish between appropriate and inappropriate behavior
PS:A1.9	Demonstrate cooperative behavior in groups
PS:A1.10	Identify personal strengths and assets
PS:A1.11	Identify and discuss changing personal and social roles
PS:A2	**Acquire Interpersonal Skills**
PS:A2.1	Recognize that everyone has rights and responsibilities
PS:A2.2	Respect alternative points of view
PS:A2.6	Use effective communications skills
PS:A2.8	Learn how to make and keep friends
Standard B: Students will make decisions, set goals and take necessary action to achieve goals.	
PS:B1	**Self-Knowledge Application**
PS:B1.1	Use a decision-making and problem-solving model
PS:B1.3	Identify alternative solutions to a problem
PS:B1.4	Develop effective coping skills for dealing with problems
PS:B1.6	Know how to apply conflict resolution skills
PS:B1.9	Identify long- and short-term goals
PS:B1.10	Identify alternative ways of achieving goals
PS:B1.12	Develop an action plan to set and achieve realistic goals
Standard C: Students will understand safety and survival skills.	
PS:C1	**Acquire Personal Safety Skills**
PS:C1.7	Apply effective problem-solving and decision-making skills to make safe and healthy choices
PS:C1.9	Learn how to cope with peer pressure
PS:C1.10	Learn techniques for managing stress and conflict

Taken From:
American School Counselor Association (2004). ASCA National Standards for Students. Alexandria, VA: Copyright 2004 by the American School Counselor Association

SESSIONS ORGANIZED BY PILLAR

1 SELF-ESTEEM BUILDING	2 LEADERSHIP SKILLS	3 COMMUNITY BUILDING
Identifying Role Models SESSION 6	Qualities Of A Leader SESSION 2	Establishing Group Norms SESSION 1
Defining Self SESSION 7	Goal Setting SESSION 5	Cooperation Within The Group SESSION 3
Health Inside & Out SESSION 8	First Impressions SESSION 11	Conflict Resolution SESSION 4
Etiquette SESSION 9	Public Speaking SESSION 12	School-Wide Cooperation SESSION 10
Celebrating Success SESSION 15	Career Exploration SESSION 13	Cooperation For A Greater Good SESSION 14

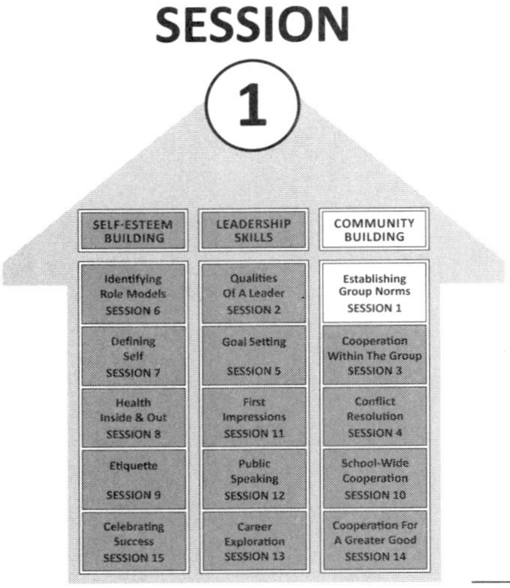

PILLAR 3
COMMUNITY BUILDING

SKILL 1: ESTABLISHING GROUP NORMS

Goal: Through group discussion, students and coordinators will review expectations and establish program norms and rules.

MATERIALS NEEDED:

For the leader:
- ☐ Banner paper or several sheets of poster board
- ☐ Marker

For each student:
- ☐ 5 sticky notes
- ☐ Marker
- ☐ *A Letter To Myself* (page 18)
- ☐ Pencil or pen
- ☐ Envelope
- ☐ Program folder or binder

INSPIRATIONAL QUOTE

I've learned that people will forget what you said, people will forget what you did, but people will never forget how you made them feel.

~ Maya Angelou, author

PRESENTATION:

STEP 1—ICEBREAKER

Begin with this icebreaker, which allows each student to share information about herself:

You Think You Know Me: Students sit in a circle. As a personal introduction, each student completes the following sentences:

My name is ______________________________ .
You may know that I ___________________________ .
You probably didn't know that I ____________________ .

STEP 2—REVIEW THE PURPOSE OF THE GROUP

Pillar 1 – Learning About Yourself
Pillar 2 – Learning To Be A Leader
Pillar 3 – Learning To Get Along With Others

STEP 3—GUIDED DISCUSSION OF EXPECTATIONS

Inform the students that today's discussion will be about how they hope to benefit from participating in this program. Ask them to think about what made them decide to join; what they hope to do, try, or experience as part of this group; and what changes they would like to see in themselves as a result of participating in this program.

Using a marker, each student writes on each of the five sticky notes one way she hopes to benefit from this program.

Label a sheet of banner paper or several sheets of poster board with these categories: *Make New Friends, Learn About Myself, Make Better Choices, Learn About Growing Into A Young Lady, Learn How To Get Along With Others, Become A Student Leader, Have Fun,* and *Other*.

The students place each sticky note in the category that most relates to what they wrote. To lead a discussion of what this activity tells us about group members' expectations, ask:

1. *Where were most of the sticky notes placed?*
2. *What do most students want to get out of this group?*
3. *How does it feel to know that many of the people here want the same things from this group that you do?*
4. *Which expectations in the* Other *category do you think we can realize this year?*

STEP 4—ESTABLISHING GROUP RULES

Explain that in order for this program to meet its goals, the members must agree to some group rules. Allow students to suggest rules they feel would be beneficial to the group. Suggest the following rules to cover everything discussed:

Respect For Members: listening to others, respecting confidentiality, and showing kindness
Respect For Group Coordinators: listening to the adults and following directions
Respect For Self: treating yourself well by taking full advantage of this program

ASSESSMENT—LETTER TO THE FUTURE YOU

Distribute *A Letter To Myself,* pencils or pens, and envelopes. Each student writes a letter to herself that she will read at the end of the school year. Instruct the students to think of what they want to get out of this program, what they are willing to put into it, and in what ways they want to grow this year. Collect the completed letters, which students have placed in sealed envelopes. Save them to redistribute at the conclusion of the school year or instruct students to place the completed letters in their program folders or binders.

A Letter To Myself

Dear ____,

I want to tell you my hopes for you for this school year.

Sincerely,

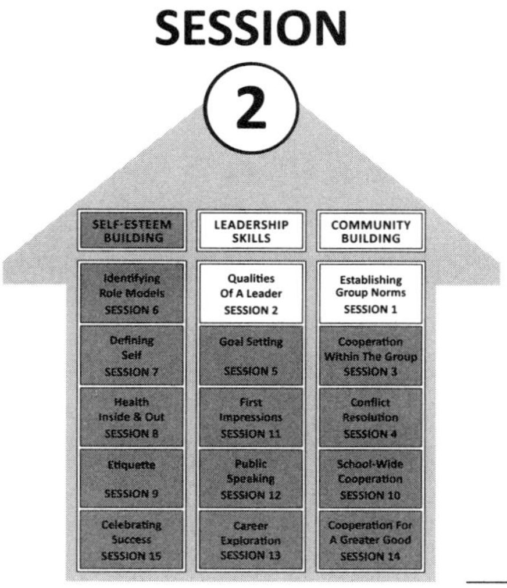

PILLAR 2
LEADERSHIP SKILLS

SKILL 1: QUALITIES OF A LEADER

Goal: Through group discussion, members will explore leadership qualities in order to determine the characteristics of a positive leader.

MATERIALS NEEDED:

For the leader:

- ☐ Invite guest speaker to talk about leadership skills
- ☐ Board or chart paper
- ☐ Marker

For each student:

- ☐ *Leadership In Action* (page 21)
- ☐ Pencil or pen
- ☐ Program folder or binder

PRESENTATION:

STEP 1—ICEBREAKER

Begin with this icebreaker, which requires students to work cooperatively:

> ***The Human Knot***: Form circles of 5–10 students. Each girl places her right arm into the circle and reaches across and holds another student's hand. Then each student extends her left arm into the circle and holds a different student's left hand. At this point, each student should be holding a hand of two different students. Explain that the students have formed a human knot and must work together to untangle themselves without anyone letting go. Observe as students discuss how to solve the problem and give directions to one another as they work to untangle their knot.

Conclude this activity by asking students what they saw, heard, or felt that indicated that someone was demonstrating good leadership skills.

STEP 2—INTRODUCE THE GUEST SPEAKER

Introduce the speaker by describing such qualifications as running her own company or being in a leadership position at her company. Tell the group that today's session will focus on the *qualities of leadership*. Explain that the speaker will talk about the personal traits she needed to become a successful leader.

SUGGESTED READING

Letters To A Young Sister

~ Hill Harper

STEP 3—DISCUSSION OF GUEST SPEAKER'S PRESENTATION

The students restate the leadership qualities they heard the guest speaker describe. List their answers on the board or chart paper. Ask the students to discuss the following questions:

1. *What trait do you think was most important? Why?*
2. *Pick a trait. How can you tell whether a person possesses or does not possess this trait?*
3. *Pick a trait. Explain how you embody this trait in everyday life.*

ASSESSMENT—LEADERSHIP IN ACTION

Distribute *Leadership In Action* and pencils or pens. Students think of ways they can use positive leadership skills in their everyday lives and complete *Leadership In Action*. To lead a discussion of students' responses, say:

1. *Share one of your sentences and explain why you feel this is a good way to show leadership.*
2. *Which two or three of your ideas can you put into practice today?*
3. *Which of your ideas would be harder for you to practice? What might make those ideas more challenging?*

Students may place the completed *Leadership In Action* in their folders or take the assignment home.

LEADERSHIP IN ACTION

How can you use positive leadership skills every day? Fill in the blanks in each statement, using selections from the word banks or adding your own.

1

respect
responsibility
creativity
good judgment
cooperation
organization
independence
kindness
fairness

2

in the classroom
in the hallways
in the cafeteria
in the bathrooms
on the bus
when I have a problem
with my family
with my friends
in my neighborhood

3

Finish the statement by writing your own idea below.

I can show____________ ________________**by** ________________________.

I can show____________ ________________**by** ________________________.

I can show____________ ________________**by** ________________________.

I can show____________ ________________**by** ________________________.

I can show____________ ________________**by** ________________________.

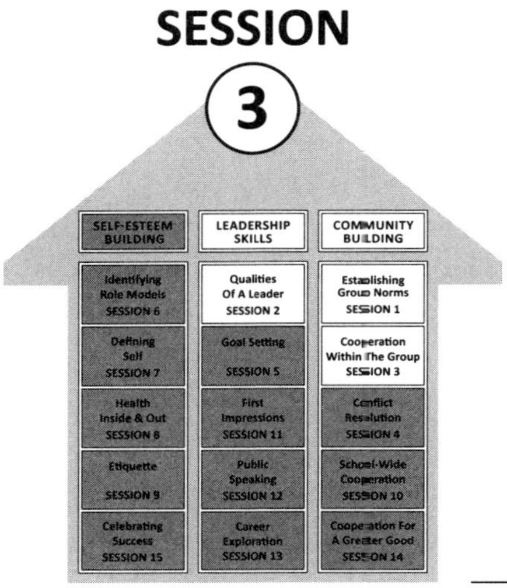

PILLAR 3
COMMUNITY BUILDING

SKILL 2: COOPERATION WITHIN THE GROUP

Goal: Students will explore the need for positive communication skills and develop the ability to cooperate by participating in low ropes course activities.

MATERIALS NEEDED:

For the leader:

☐ Milk crate or a similar sturdy wooden box for every 6 students

For each student:

☐ Program folder or binder

For each student group:

☐ *Working Together: What I Saw* (page 24)
☐ *Working Together: What I Heard* (page 25)
☐ *Working Together: What I Felt* (page 26)
☐ Pencil or pen
☐ Toothpicks (1 box for every group of 3 students)
☐ Marshmallows (1 bag for every group of 3 students)

PRESENTATION:

STEP 1—ICEBREAKER

Begin with this icebreaker, which requires students to work cooperatively:

> ***Silent Line-Up***: Instruct the students that the entire group will need to line up according to last names. Students may use non-verbal communication, but may not use words to find their place in the line.

Debrief by asking what students saw, heard, or felt that indicated they were working well together as a group.

STEP 2—EVERYONE ON THE BOX

Organize students into groups of six. Tell the students that their challenge is to get all six members of their group standing with both feet on the box long enough to recite the alphabet. Observe as the students complete this challenge. Debrief by asking what students had to do to work together effectively. Distribute one copy of *Working Together: What I Saw/Heard/Felt* and pencils or pens to each student group. Instruct the students to write their responses in the appropriate categories on the activity sheets. For example, on:

> *What I Saw* they could write what they saw students doing (taking turns, helping someone, etc.)
>
> *What I Heard* they could write what they heard (good job, nice try, etc.)
>
> *What I Felt* they could write what they felt (included, respected, listened to, etc.)

STEP 3—TOOTHPICK TOWERS

Divide students into groups of three to use their marshmallows and toothpicks to create the largest tower that can stand on its own. Assign one member of each group to be in charge of watching for what demonstrates cooperation, one to listen for things, and one to observe feelings. Give the groups four minutes to plan their structure and six minutes for building.

ASSESSMENT—DEBRIEF TOOTHPICK TOWERS

Ask what indications of cooperation students saw, heard, or felt and how they could apply their cooperation skills in school, at home, or in their neighborhood.

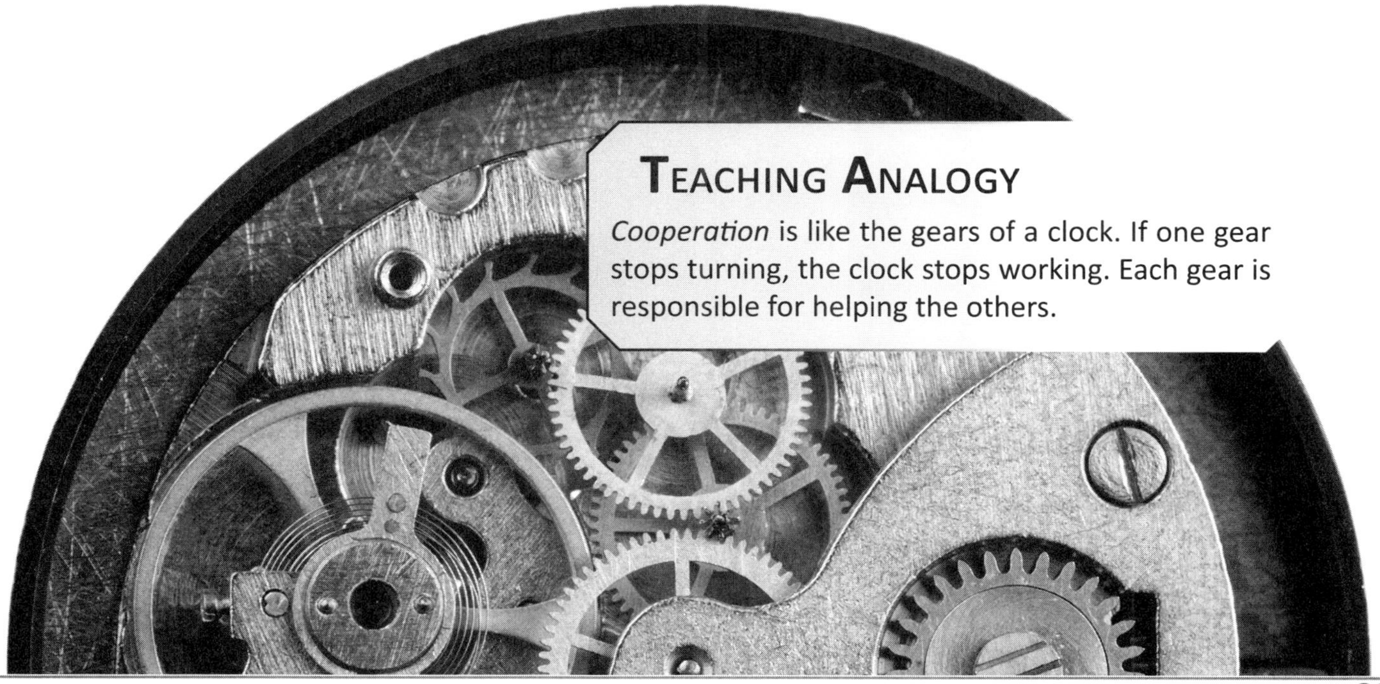

What I

Saw

What I

Heard

What I

Felt

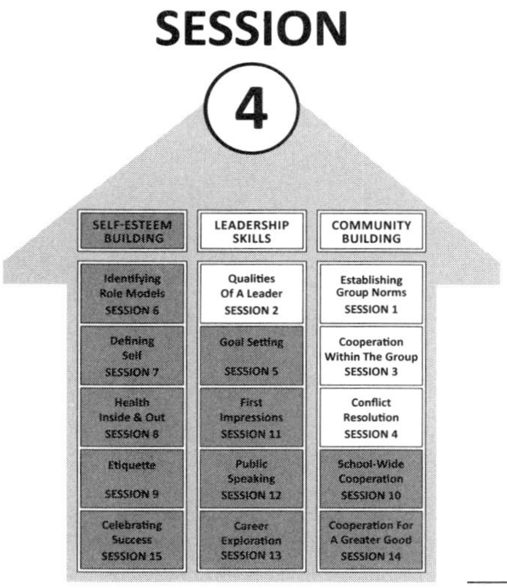

PILLAR 3
COMMUNITY BUILDING

SKILL 3: CONFLICT RESOLUTION

Goal: Through role-play, group members will develop conflict-resolution skills and learn to resolve disputes peacefully.

MATERIALS NEEDED:

For each student:

- ☐ *Conflict Resolution 1—My Story* (page 33)
- ☐ *Conflict Resolution 2—My Story* (page 34)
- ☐ Pen or pencil
- ☐ Program folder or binder

For each student group leader:

- ☐ *Understanding Perspective* (pages 29-32)

PRESENTATION:

What do you see in this picture?

STEP 1—ICEBREAKER

Begin with an icebreaker that relates to understanding perspectives:

What do YOU See?: Place three student volunteers in different parts of the room: one standing where the adult/teacher might stand, another standing where a student might stand, and a third standing with her forehead against a wall in a corner of the room. Each student describes what she sees. Explain that each person sees the same room a little differently. Two students who have a problem or disagreement can see the same conflict in very different ways. Explain that today's activities will help group members better understand how to relate to a different perspective and resolve conflicts peacefully.

STEP 2—UNDERSTANDING PERSPECTIVE

Organize students into groups of five. Each group completes all four *Understanding Perspective* activity sheets, then shares its responses with the class.

ASSESSMENT—CONFLICT RESOLUTION—MY STORY

Distribute *Conflict Resolution 1—My Story* and pencils or pens. Students complete the activity sheet which requires them to write about a conflict they had with another person. If things did not turn out as well as they wanted, ask what they might have done differently to resolve that conflict peacefully. Students may place their completed *Conflict Resolution* papers in their program folder or take them home.

Distribute *Conflict Resolution 2—My Story.* Encourage students to use the activity sheet to find a positive resolution the next time they have a dispute with a peer.

UNDERSTANDING PERSPECTIVE

Battling For A Basketball

Kierstin and Sean both like playing basketball at recess, but there is only one basketball for the kids to share. This is what Kierstin and Sean had to say:

Kierstin's Story

I like to play basketball with my friends during recess. There's only one basketball. So as soon as Mrs. Keith puts the ball out, I run over to get it. Sean got there at the same time I did yesterday, but I got the ball first. He took the ball from me and ran away. I was angry and embarrassed! My friends were laughing because he stole the ball from me! He fell when I tried to take it back. Then I had to go to the principal's office. Sean didn't get into trouble, and I don't think that's fair.

Sean's Story

Every day at recess, Kierstin runs and gets the basketball. I try to get there first, but she's always a little faster. So yesterday I asked if I could play with her and her friends. She said *no*. I was embarrassed that she would laugh at me in front of everyone, so I took the ball from her. She chased me and pushed me to the ground. Mrs. Keith saw what happened and sent Kierstin to the principal's office.

Kierstin's Perspective

What feelings did Kierstin have?

____

Why is Kierstin upset?

____

____

Sean's Perspective

What feelings did Sean have?

____

Why is Sean upset?

____

____

What could Kierstin and Sean do to fix this situation?

Kierstin could ______________________________

____

Sean could ______________________________

____

UNDERSTANDING PERSPECTIVE

The Case Of The Broken Volcano

Melissa and Trevaughn are in Mr. Park's science class and each of them spent a month working on a project. On the day the projects were due, Melissa's got broken. This is what they had to say:

Melissa's Story

I worked hard on my science project, a huge volcano with orange and red lava, and was proud of how great it turned out. Trevaughn asked if he could pick it up. I said *no*. He picked it up anyway, and dropped it when I tried to get it back. It broke into a million pieces, and the lava inside went everywhere. I'm so angry at Trevaughn for breaking my project! Why couldn't he just leave it alone?

Trevaughn's Story

Our science projects were due today. Melissa wanted to see my tomato plant, so I let her hold it. But when I started to pick up her volcano, she shouted *no!* at me. Before I could put it down, she tried to grab it. I lost my grip and it fell. I felt bad that it was broken, but I don't know why Melissa had to yell at me. I just wanted to look at it.

Melissa's Perspective

What feelings did Melissa have?

____

Why is Melissa upset?

____

____

Trevaughn's Perspective

What feelings did Trevaughn have?

____

Why is Trevaughn upset?

____

____

What could Melissa and Trevaughn do to fix this situation?

Melissa could ______________________________

____

Trevaughn could ______________________________

____

UNDERSTANDING PERSPECTIVE

The Trouble With Rumors

Stephanie and Shavon were best friends. That changed when someone started a rumor about Stephanie. This is what they had to say:

Stephanie's Story

Shavon used to be my best friend. We did everything together. Then my friend Sam told me Shavon told people that I cheated on a math test. I got the highest grade in the class and was really excited! Shavon knows I didn't cheat. I was hurt and sad when I found out what she was saying that about me. When I asked why she would spread a rumor about me, she said she didn't. I can't believe my best friend would do that to me!

Shavon's Story

Stephanie and I were best friends. Then one day, she asked me why I started a rumor about her. I told her I didn't. She said she heard that I was telling people she cheated on a test. I would never say that about Stephanie. I tried to tell her it was a lie, but she wouldn't believe me. I'm sad and hurt because I feel like I don't have a best friend any more.

Stephanie's Perspective

What feelings did Stephanie have?

____

Why is Stephanie upset?

____

____

Shavon's Perspective

What feelings did Shavon have?

____

Why is Shavon upset?

____

____

What could Stephanie and Shavon do to fix this situation?

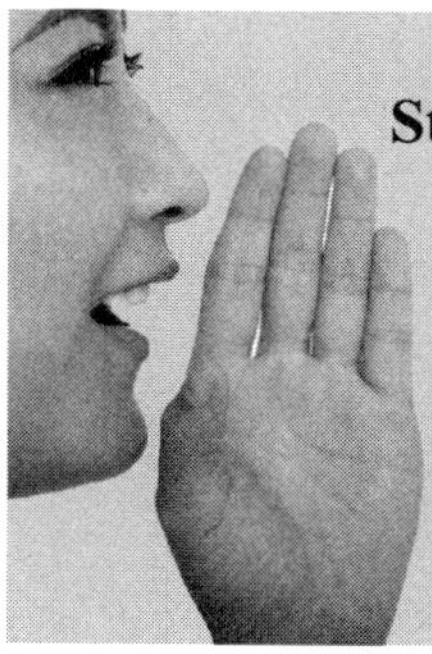

Stephanie could ______________________________

____

Shavon could ______________________________

____

UNDERSTANDING PERSPECTIVE

Weird Science

Katlin and JR are lab partners in science. They had a fight over supplies. This is what they had to say:

Katlin's Story

Science is my favorite subject, so I was excited to be learning about chemicals. My mom let me bring some glass bottles, baking soda, and food coloring to use in class. When I started mixing the chemicals, JR wanted to do it. I said he would have to wait. He said that wasn't fair and called me a jerk. It made me angry when he called me a name just because I wouldn't let him hold my stuff. I don't want to be JR's partner any more.

JR's Story

I like learning about chemicals, because mixing different things together is fun. Today, Katlin brought in extra stuff that her Mom gave her. She was mixing water and food coloring. It looked like fun, so I asked if I could try. Katlin said it was her stuff and I couldn't have a turn. I was disappointed, because I wanted to try, too. Katlin said I should ask my mom to buy me my own. That made me angry. I don't want to be Katlin's partner any more.

Katlin's Perspective

What feelings did Katlin have?

____

Why is Katlin upset?

____

____

JR's Perspective

What feelings did JR have?

____

Why is JR upset?

____

____

What could Katlin and JR do to fix this situation?

Katlin could ________________________________

____

JR could ________________________________

____

CONFLICT RESOLUTION 1

My Story

Think about a time you had a conflict with another person. Use the space below to write about your conflict and how you could have resolved it.

My Perspective

What feelings did I have?

____

Why was I upset?

____

____

The Other Person's Story

What feelings did he/she have?

____

Why was he/she upset?

____

____

What could we each have done to fix this situation?

I could have ______________________________

____

The other person could have ______________________________

____

CONFLICT RESOLUTION 2

My Story

I have a conflict with another person. This is what happened and how we may be able to resolve it.

My Story

The Other Person's Story

My Perspective

What feelings do I have?

____

Why am I upset?

____

____

The Other Person's Story

What feelings does he/she have?

____

Why is he/she upset?

____

____

What could we each do to fix this situation?

I could______________________________

____

The other person could______________________________

____

SESSION

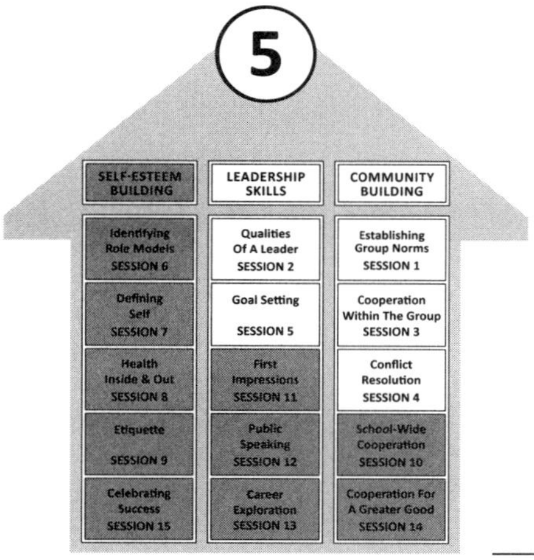

PILLAR 2
LEADERSHIP SKILLS

SKILL 2: GOAL SETTING

Goal: By completing goal sheets, students will establish personal, academic and/or behavioral goals and develop the ability to monitor long-term and short-term goals.

MATERIALS NEEDED:

For the leader:

- ☐ Multiple copies of *Raising The Bar* (page 44)

For each student:

- ☐ *Setting Personal Goals: Sprint Goals* (page 37)
- ☐ *Setting Personal Goals: Marathon Goals* (page 38)
- ☐ *Future Fair Project* (pages 39-43)
- ☐ Pencil or pen
- ☐ Poster or display boards, markers, glue, scissors, construction paper, and access to a computer room
- ☐ Program folder or binder

PRESENTATION:

STEP 1—ICEBREAKER

Begin with this icebreaker, which allows students to discuss different types of goals:

> ***Goal Setting***: Lead a discussion of goals by asking students to think about the following questions:
>
> 1. *What is a* goal?
> 2. *What is the difference between long-term and short-term goals?*
> 3. *What is a* measurable goal? (How can you tell when you've reached a goal?)
> 4. *What traits does a person need to reach long-term goals?*

STEP 2—ADDRESSING OBSTACLES TO SUCCESS

Distribute *Setting Personal Goals: Sprint Goals, Setting Personal Goals: Marathon Goals,* and pencils or pens. After students complete *Sprint Goals* and *Marathon Goals,* discuss their answers and ideas for how to address obstacles they might find in their path to success.

ASSESSMENT—FUTURE FAIR PROJECT

Tell students they will complete an assignment similar to a science fair project, but will be researching their own future. Provide pages 39-43 and the supplies listed in the *Materials Needed* section. Help students complete each project section and assemble their project boards. It may take several sessions and work at home to complete this assignment. Consider scheduling a time for students to show their projects to parents, other students, and/or school staff.

ALTERNATE ASSESSMENT—RAISING THE BAR

Distribute copies of *Raising The Bar* to each student. Encourage group members to set a goal grade for each of their classes and to use *Raising The Bar* to chart their grades at the end of each quarter. Use the interim columns for recording important grades made during the quarter. If a student's grade has fallen below her goal, discuss a plan for getting back to the desired level.

Students may place this lesson's completed assignments in their program folder or take them home.

Extending the Lesson

Consider scheduling a field trip to an area college. Allowing group members to see a college campus can help them visualize their goals for higher education.

OR

Invite college students to talk to group members about the importance of setting goals and making plans to accomplish them.

Setting Personal Goals:
SPRINT GOALS

A **sprint goal** is something you would like to accomplish in a week, in a month, or maybe by the end of the school year.

OBSTACLES:
Name three problems that could make it hard for you to achieve your sprint goals.

1.

2.

3.

FINISH LINE: Describe what you would like to accomplish.

Setting Personal Goals: MARATHON GOALS

A **marathon goal** is something you would like to accomplish in the next 10 to 20 years.

These goals help you determine what you want for your future.

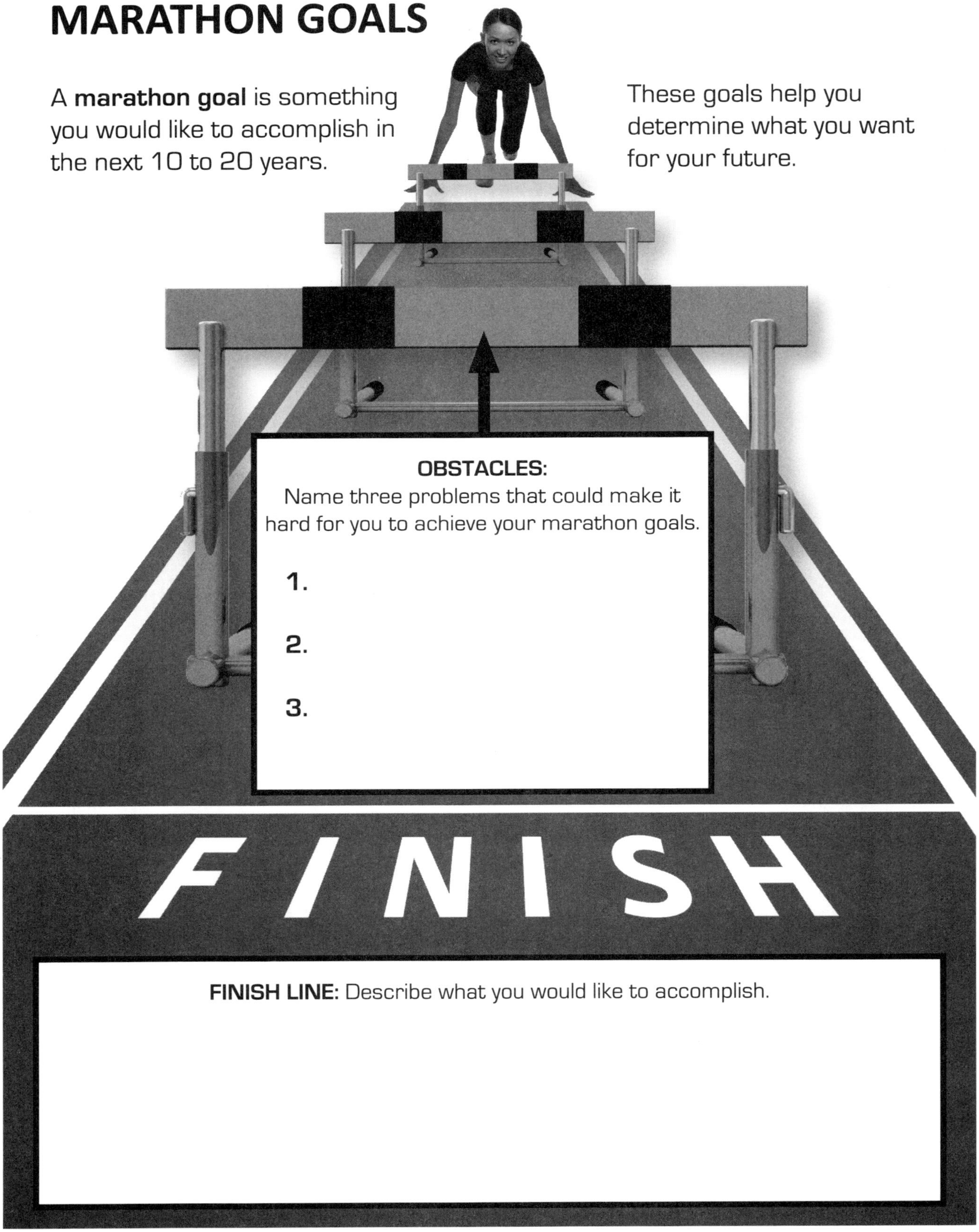

OBSTACLES:
Name three problems that could make it hard for you to achieve your marathon goals.

1.

2.

3.

FINISH LINE: Describe what you would like to accomplish.

FUTURE FAIR PROJECT

STEP 1:
Choose A Career

STEP 2:
Write Your Essay

STEP 3:
Conduct Your Research

STEP 4:
Identify Supporting Objects & Documents

STEP 1: Career Goal Statement

Please write a career goal that you have.
Write about what you will need to do to achieve this goal.

Write an essay that tells about how your life will be in 15 years. Answer the following questions:

- What career will you have?
- What will your family look like?
- Where will you live?
- What will you do for fun?
- How will you have changed as a person?
- How will the world have changed because of you?

STEP 2:
My Life In 15 Years

STEP 3: Research

YOUR CAREER CHOICE ______________________

Research Sources

List four websites/books/magazines/journals you used to conduct your research:

____

____

____

____

Responsibilities

List four things a person in this career must do every day:

____

____

____

____

Salary

What is the average salary for this career?

____

High School

What high school courses might be helpful to a person who wants to have this career?

____

____

____

____

After High School

Is training other than high school needed to do this job?

____

____

____

____

College

What degree or degrees are needed to do this work?

____

____

____

List three colleges that offer training for this career:

____

____

____

STEP 4: Supporting Items & Documents

Where can you find items and documents to use in your *Future Fair Display*?

PICTURES

What pictures would you like to include?	Where can you find them?
______________________	______________________
______________________	______________________
______________________	______________________
______________________	______________________

ESSAYS/ARTICLES

What documents can you include?	Where can you find them?
______________________	______________________
______________________	______________________
______________________	______________________
______________________	______________________

OBJECTS

What objects would you like to include?	Where can you find them?
______________________	______________________
______________________	______________________
______________________	______________________
______________________	______________________

MEDIA

What music/video would you like to include?	Where can you find them?
______________________	______________________
______________________	______________________
______________________	______________________
______________________	______________________

What other media would you like to include?	Where can you find them?
______________________	______________________
______________________	______________________
______________________	______________________

RAISING THE BAR

SUBJECT:

	GOAL		INTERIM 1	REPORT CARD Q1	INTERIM 2	REPORT CARD Q2	INTERIM 3	REPORT CARD Q3	INTERIM 4	REPORT CARD Q4
A										
B										
C										
D										
E										

SUBJECT:

	GOAL		INTERIM 1	REPORT CARD Q1	INTERIM 2	REPORT CARD Q2	INTERIM 3	REPORT CARD Q3	INTERIM 4	REPORT CARD Q4
A										
B										
C										
D										
E										

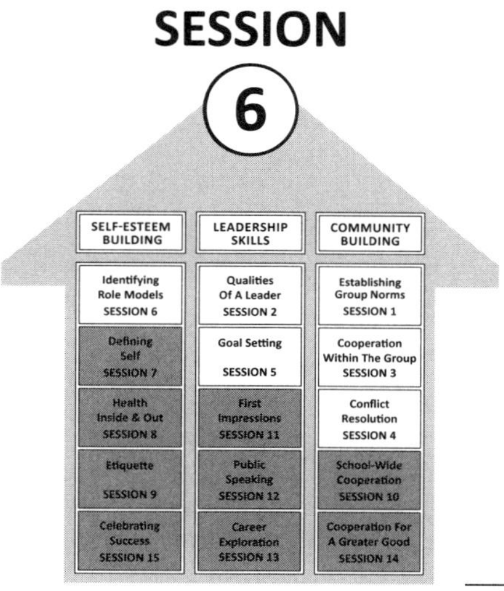

PILLAR 1
SELF-ESTEEM BUILDING

SKILL 1: IDENTIFYING ROLE MODELS

Goal: Through completion of guided projects, students will identify and define the qualities of a positive role model by examining lives of women in media, in history, and in their own lives.

MATERIALS NEEDED:

For the leader:

- ☐ Photographs of 5 or more inspiring women posted on wall or board
- ☐ Tape
- ☐ Access to a computer lab or library, or a collection of biographies of women in history

For each student:

- ☐ *Great Women In History* (page 47)
- ☐ *I Admire...* (page 48)
- ☐ Sticky notes
- ☐ Pencil or pen
- ☐ Envelope (optional)
- ☐ Program folder or binder

PRESENTATION:

STEP 1—ICEBREAKER

Distribute pencils or pens and sticky notes. Begin with this icebreaker, which requires students to think about women they admire:

> ***Women I Admire***: If every girl in the group is not familiar with most or all of the women whose pictures you've posted on the wall or board, briefly describe each one. Group members think about words to describe each woman, write these words on sticky notes, then post them around the appropriate picture.

Discuss students' answers to the following questions:

1. *Pick a person. Why do you think people describe this person with the words listed?*

2. *What words have been used to describe more than one person?*
3. *Which of these words do you feel suggest that person would be a good role model?*

STRENGTH IN NUMBERS

You can help your students learn about positive role models by helping them find one. Ask staff members to mentor individual group members.
OR
Contact local businesses and ask if women who work there would serve as mentor pen-pals to students.

STEP 2—GREAT WOMEN IN HISTORY

Distribute *Great Women in History*. Allow students time to read the sheet and research their answers. When everyone has finished, each student tells the group what she learned about the woman she chose to research.

ASSESSMENT—I ADMIRE

Distribute *I Admire…* . Students complete the activity sheet by writing about women they admire. You may encourage group members to write personal letters letting women they admire know why they consider them positive role models.

Students may place completed assignments in their program folder or take them home.

Great Women In History

PLEASE SELECT A WOMAN FROM HISTORY:

When was she born? ______________________________

Where did she grow up? ______________________________

What made her great? ______________________________

What obstacles did she have to overcome? ______________________________

In what ways are you like the person you selected? ______________________________

If this woman could advise young women at your school, what do you think she would say?

I Admire...

Think about women you admire.

They may be celebrities, women from history, or women you know personally. What characteristics or qualities make them good role models for you? Write about these women below.

I ADMIRE

because ______________________________

____

____

____

____

I ADMIRE

because ______________________________

____

____

____

____

I ADMIRE

because ______________________________

____

____

____

____

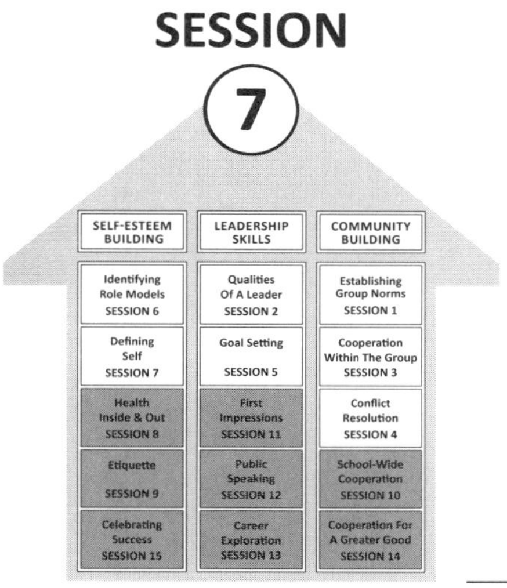

PILLAR 1
SELF-ESTEEM BUILDING

SKILL 2: DEFINING SELF

Goal: Group members participate in discussion to learn about positive character traits and determine their own personal strengths.

MATERIALS NEEDED:

For the leader:

- ☐ Markers or other art supplies

For each student:

- ☐ *Character Blocks* (pages 51-54)
- ☐ *Poem Of YOU* (page 55)
- ☐ Pencil or pen
- ☐ Scissors
- ☐ Glue stick
- ☐ Program folder or binder

PRESENTATION:

STEP 1—ICEBREAKER

Begin with this icebreaker, which requires students to think about personal character traits:

> ***Adjective Name Game***: Divide students into groups of approximately 10 members. Each group sits in a circle. Each group member thinks of an adjective that describes her and begins with the same letter as her first name. One person says her adjective and name, and each subsequent person says her adjective and name and those of all the group members who have gone before her.

STEP 2 – CHARACTER BLOCKS

Distribute *Character Blocks* and pencils or pens. Group members think about words that best describe them in different environments. Ask:

1. *How would people describe you at home?*
2. *How would people describe you at school?*
3. *How would your family or friends describe you?*
4. *Which character traits are you most proud of?*

Each group member writes a word she would use to describe herself in each square of each block on *Character Blocks* and decorates, cuts out, and assembles her blocks. The blank character block can be used for group members to describe another important aspect of their lives.

Divide students into groups of about five members. After each student has presented what she wrote on each block and explained why she wrote it, discuss the following questions:

1. *What character traits did we see over and over again on peoples' blocks?*
2. *Why do you think these traits are important?*
3. *What differences do we see between our traits at home, at school, or with friends?*
4. *Pick a trait. Give an example of how you demonstrate that trait at school, at home, or with your friends or family.*

ASSESSMENT—POEM OF YOU

Distribute *Poem Of YOU.* Students complete their poems, which requires them to fill in the blanks with words that describe themselves, roles they play in their lives, and personal aspirations. They may place the completed activity sheet in their program folder or take the assignment home.

Songs for Discussion

After playing India.Arie's *"Beautiful Flower"* and *"I Am Not My Hair,"* instruct students to list all the positive character traits they heard mentioned in the songs. Then discuss why each trait is important for a young woman to possess.

Character Blocks

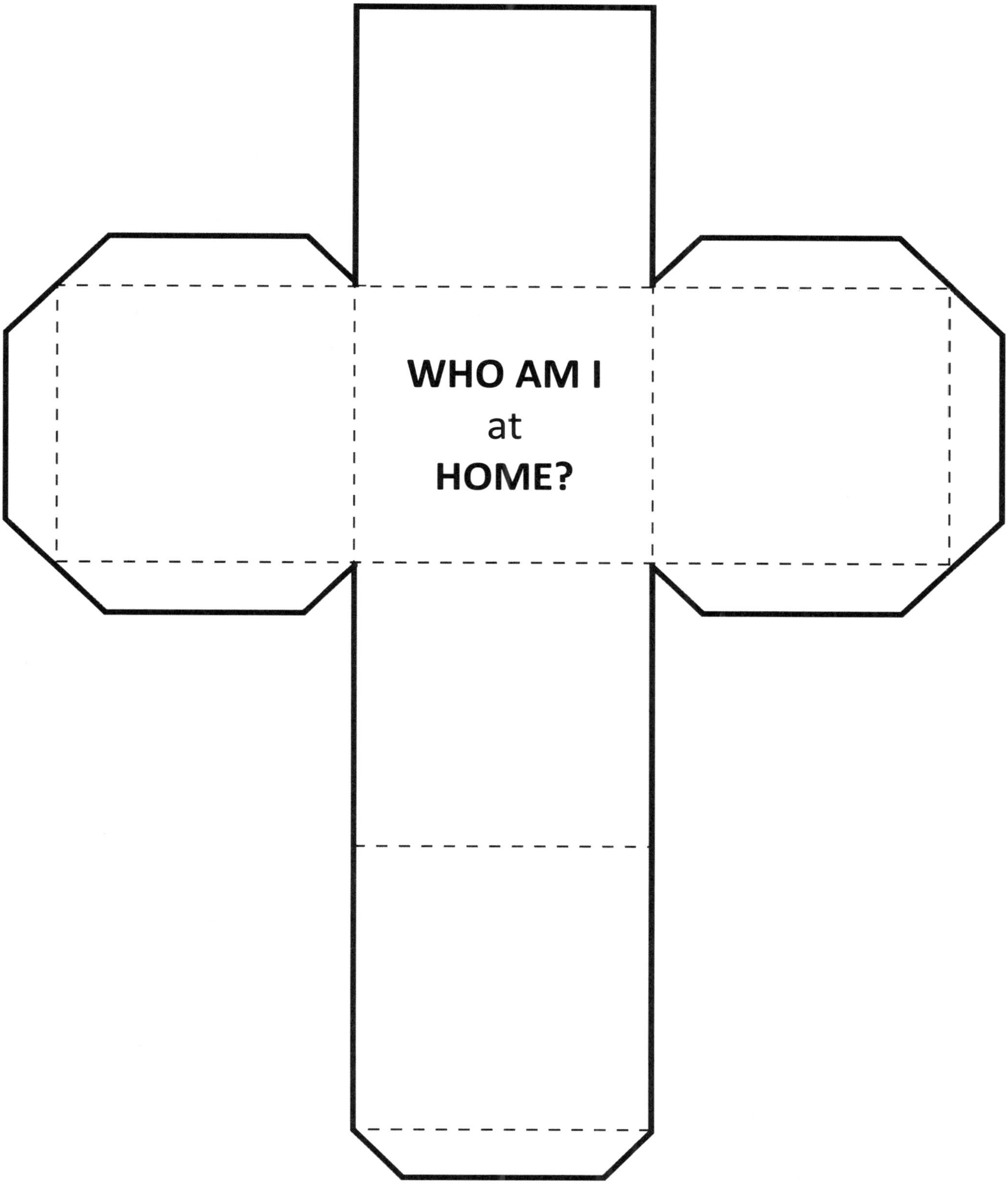

Character Blocks

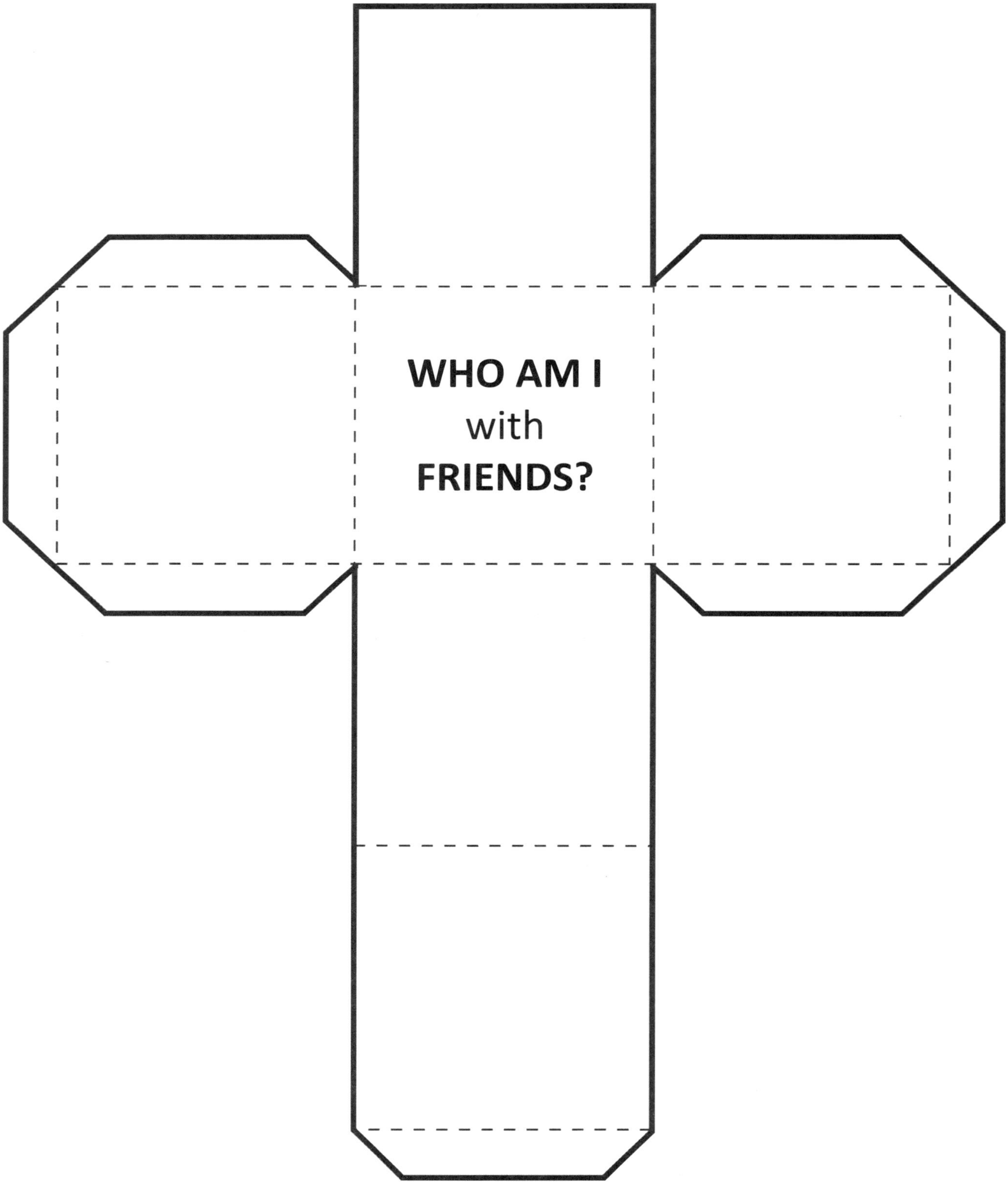

Character Blocks

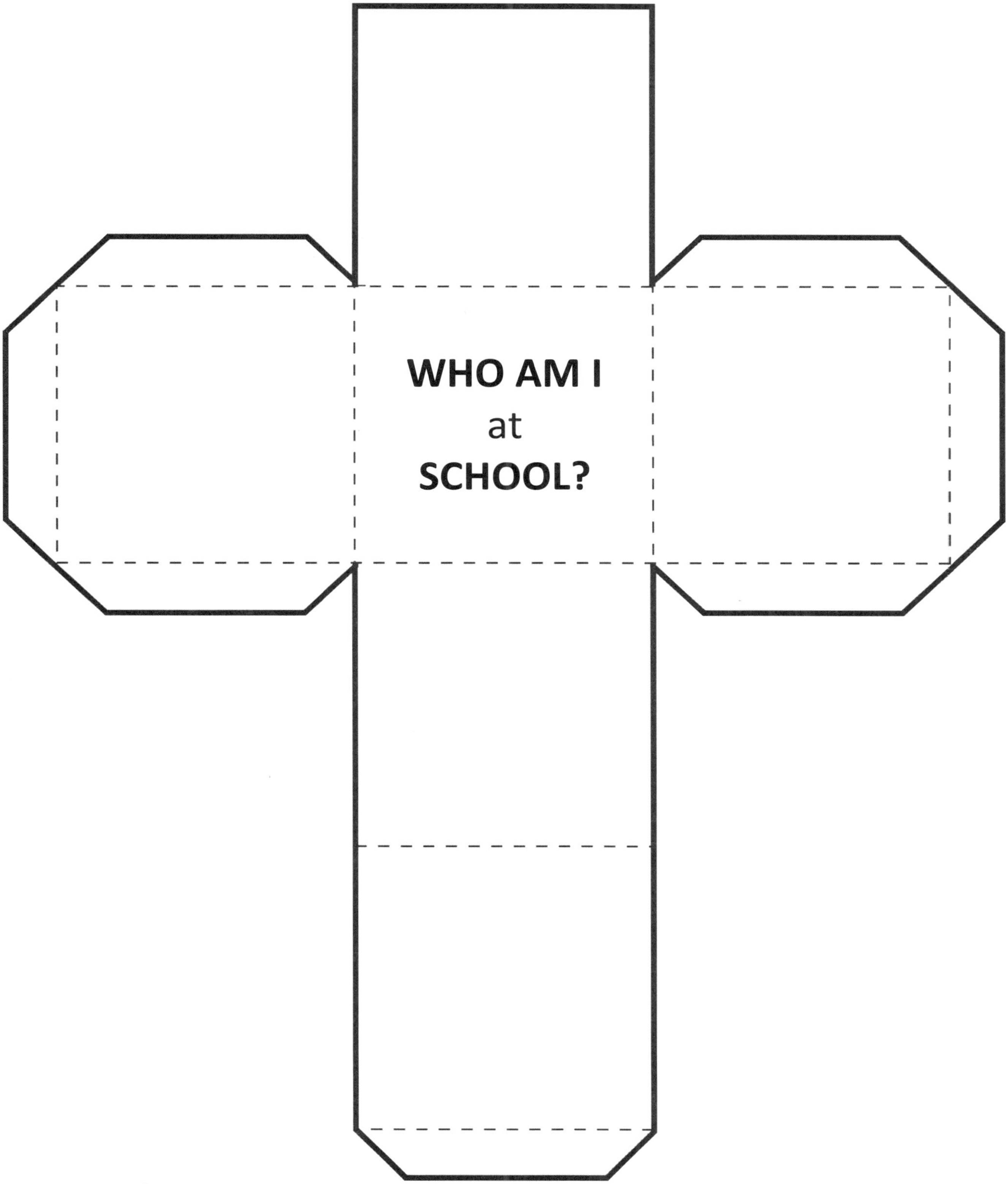

Character Blocks

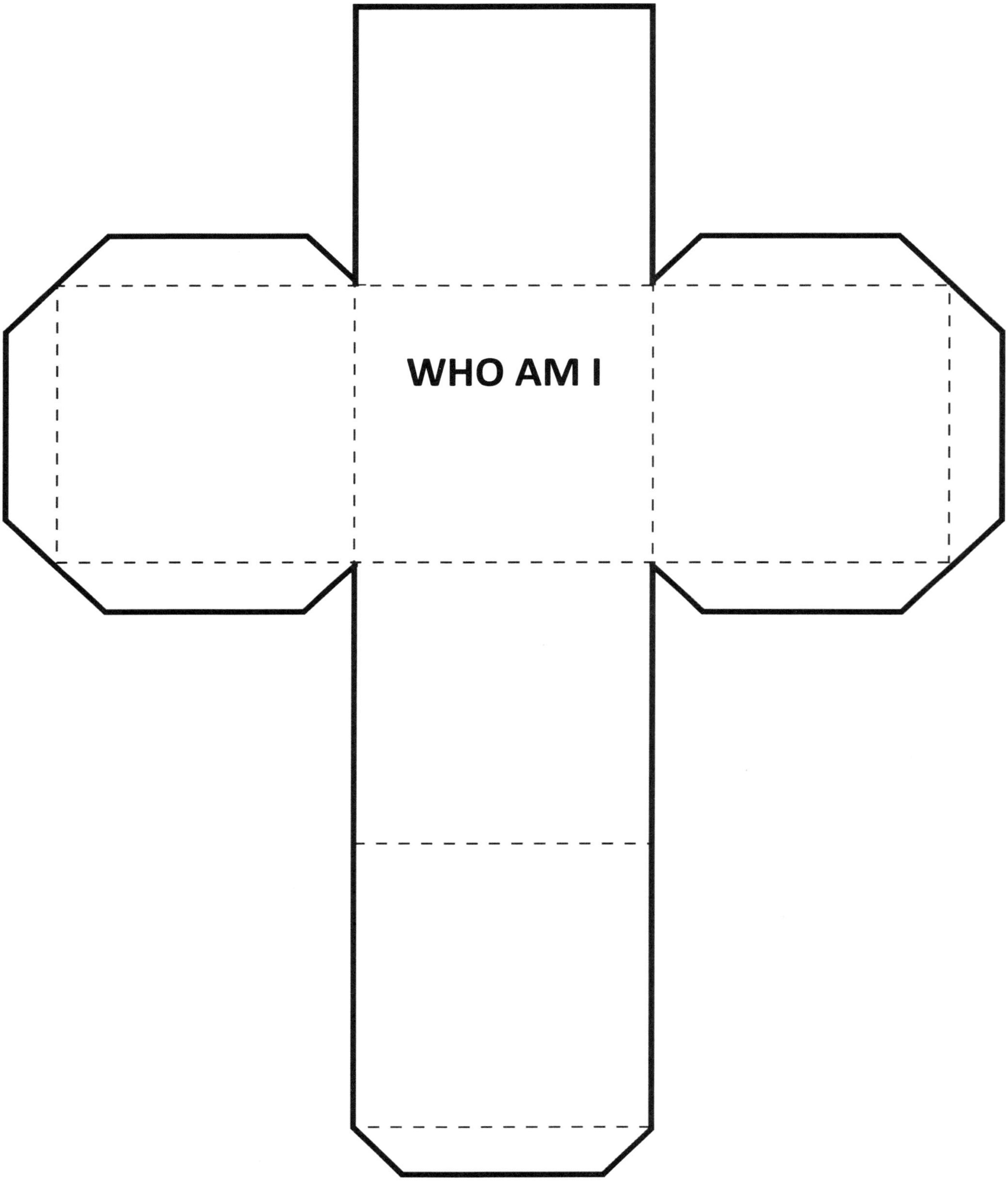

Poem Of YOU

I AM

____
YOUR FIRST NAME

I AM A

___________________ ___________________ ___________________
3 ROLES YOU HAVE

I AM

______________ ______________ ______________ ______________
4 ADJECTIVES THAT DESCRIBE YOU

I ENJOY

___________________ ___________________ ___________________
3 THINGS YOU ENJOY DOING

I WANT TO

_______________________________ _______________________________
2 THINGS YOU WANT TO DO WITH YOUR LIFE

I AM

____
YOUR FIRST AND LAST NAME

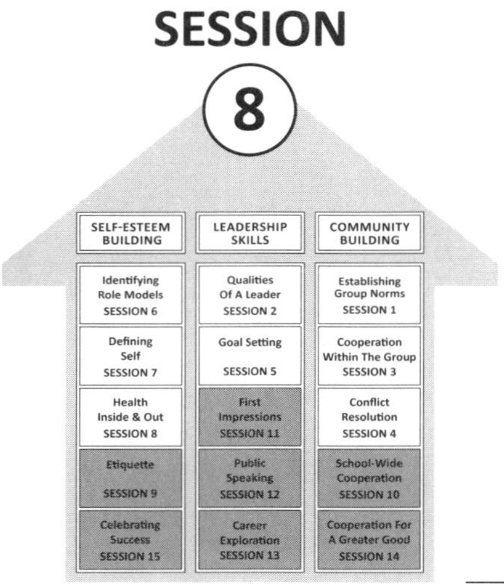

PILLAR 1
SELF-ESTEEM BUILDING

SKILL 3: HEALTH INSIDE & OUT

Goal: Students will listen to guest speakers discuss topics related to personal health and learn the importance of self-care.

MATERIALS NEEDED:

For the leader:

- ☐ Board or chart paper and marker
- ☐ Guest speakers on:
  - Physical Fitness – Ask a local gym to provide a guest speaker or invite your physical education teacher to attend.
  - Nutrition – Ask a local hospital to provide a nutritionist or invite your school nurse to attend.
  - Consider inviting additional speakers to cover such topics as skin care or (for older students) dating violence.
- ☐ Room or corner of a room for each guest speaker
- ☐ Chairs for students at each speaker's station
- ☐ Scissors

For each student:

- ☐ *Health & Wellness Fair Exit Tickets* (pages 58-59)
- ☐ Pencil or pen
- ☐ Paper
- ☐ Program folder or binder

PRESENTATION:

STEP 1—ICEBREAKER

Distribute pencils or pens and paper. Begin with this icebreaker, which requires students to think about health and wellness:

> ***Question Writing***: Inform the students that guest speakers will discuss being healthy. On the board or chart paper, list the topics that will be covered. For each topic, each student writes two questions she would like to have answered.

STEP 2—HEALTH & WELLNESS FAIR

Divide students into as many groups as the number of guest speakers. Rotate each group to a new speaker's area at the end of each 20-minute presentation. Allow time for group members to ask their prepared questions.

ASSESSMENT—HEALTH & WELLNESS FAIR EXIT TICKETS

Distribute *Health & Wellness Fair Exit Tickets*. Each student completes each ticket, which requires her to write about things she learned from the presentations and changes she will make based upon what the guest speaker said. Students may place completed *Exit Tickets* in their program folder or take the assignment home.

ARTISTIC EXPRESSION

Work with your art teacher to invite group members to create self-portraits that showcase ways that they take care of themselves inside and out.

Health & Wellness Fair Exit Tickets

SESSION TOPIC: EXERCISE

List three things you learned during this session:

____

____

____

Describe one thing you may do differently now that you've attended this session:

____

____

____

SESSION TOPIC: NUTRITION

List three things you learned during this session:

____

____

____

Describe one thing you may do differently now that you've attended this session:

____

____

____

Health & Wellness Fair Exit Tickets

SESSION TOPIC: ______________________

List three things you learned during this session:

____

____

____

Describe one thing you may do differently now that you've attended this session:

____

____

____

SESSION TOPIC: ______________________

List three things you learned during this session:

____

____

____

Describe one thing you may do differently now that you've attended this session:

____

____

____

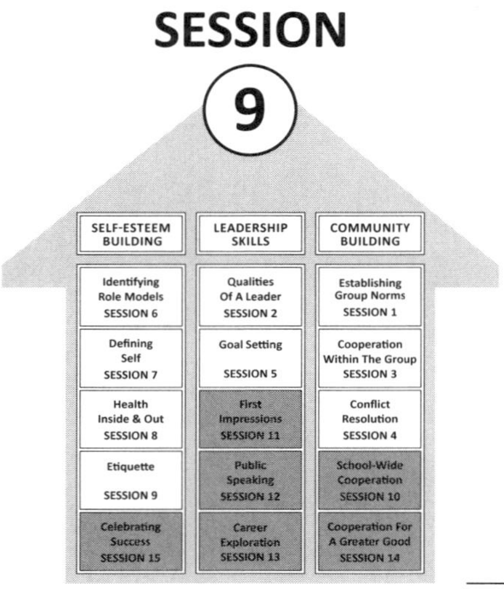

PILLAR 1
SELF-ESTEEM BUILDING

SKILL 4: ETIQUETTE

Goal: Through participation in activities, group members will explore customs and manners in order to familiarize themselves with rules of etiquette.

MATERIALS NEEDED:

For the leader:

- ☐ Group tables and chairs for all students
- ☐ Tablecloths for each table (optional)
- ☐ Refreshments (optional)

For each student:

- ☐ *Unwritten Rules* (page 62)
- ☐ *Rules Of Etiquette: Formal Dining* (page 63)
- ☐ Pencil or pen
- ☐ Napkin (paper or cloth)
- ☐ Plate (paper or formal)
- ☐ Flatware (plastic or formal)
- ☐ Program folder or binder

PRESENTATION:

STEP 1—ICEBREAKER

Distribute *Unwritten Rules* and pencils or pens. Begin with this icebreaker, which will help start a conversation about etiquette:

> ***Unwritten Rules***: Students complete *Unwritten Rules* independently, then compare responses with a partner. Debrief this activity by discussing the variety of rules students generated for different places they visit. Explain that *etiquette* means following unwritten rules. Discuss why these rules are important and what good etiquette says about a person.

STEP 2—DINNER ETIQUETTE PRACTICE

Lead the students in enacting a formal dinner. Instruct the students on how to set the tables using plates, napkins, and flatware. If you have brought refreshments, students take turns acting as servers. Visit individual tables to discuss typical rules of etiquette for a formal dinner. Instruct the students to make a mental note of every unwritten rule of etiquette they observe.

ASSESSMENT—RULES OF ETIQUETTE: FORMAL DINING

Distribute *Rules Of Etiquette: Formal Dining.* At the conclusion of your practice dinner, discuss the rules of etiquette students noted. Have them list these ideas on the *Rules Of Etiquette* sheet. Students may place their completed sheets in their program folder or take the assignment home.

Field Experience

A field trip to any of the following places allows students to apply rules of etiquette in real-life situations:

- Dinner at a restaurant
- Ballet or opera
- Museum
- Library

Unwritten Rules

Think about rules and customs for different places you might visit. Look at the list below and fill in the blanks to create rules for each place.

Where is it bad manners to:

Put your feet on the table ______________________________.

Stand up and dance ______________________________.

Call out to your friends ______________________________.

Talk with your mouth full ______________________________.

Text friends ______________________________.

Chew gum ______________________________.

Shout to get someone's attention ______________________________.

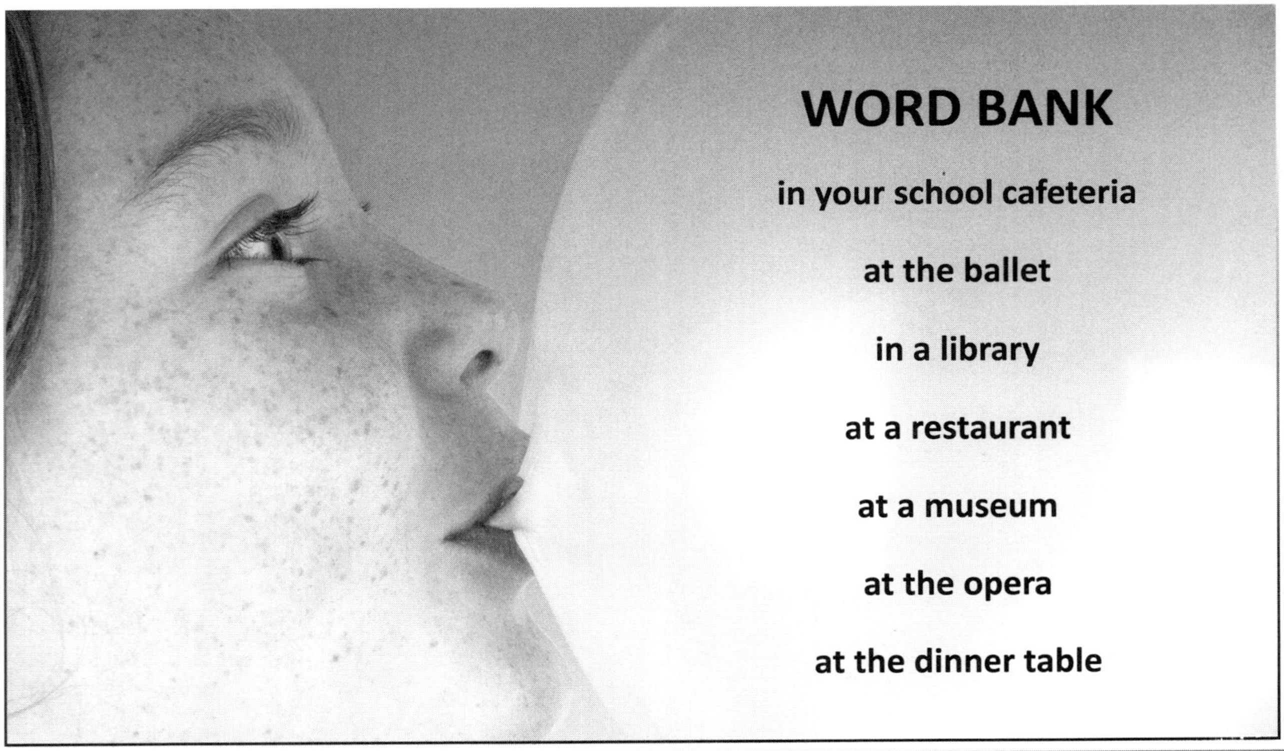

Rules Of Etiquette:
Formal Dining

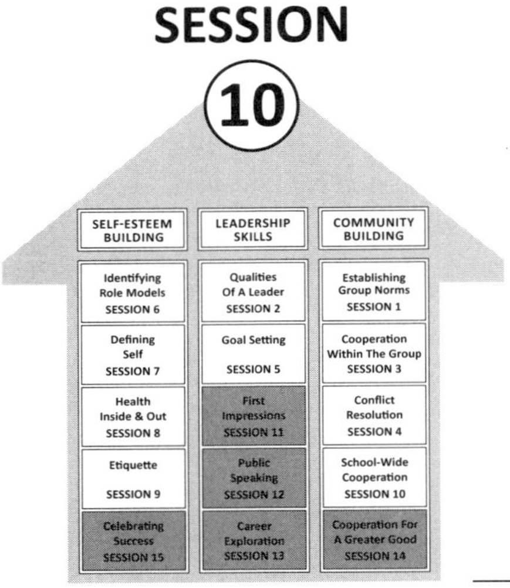

PILLAR 3
COMMUNITY BUILDING

SKILL 4: SCHOOL-WIDE COOPERATION

Goal: Students will create and organize a student-run program to encourage involvement in a positive school-wide initiative.

MATERIALS NEEDED:

For the leader:

- ☐ Construction paper cut into strips
- ☐ Scissors
- ☐ Stapler or transparent tape
- ☐ Several poster boards
- ☐ Multiple copies of *Warm Fuzzy Forms* (page 66)

For each student:

- ☐ Pencil or pen
- ☐ Markers or colored pencils
- ☐ Program folder or binder

PRESENTATION:

STEP 1—ICEBREAKERS

Distribute markers or colored pencils and construction paper strips. Begin with this icebreaker, which will help start a conversation about working together:

> ***Paper Chains***: Students think of three things they could do to improve the school. Each group member writes each response on a separate strip of construction paper. As the students finish writing, collect the construction strips and roll each into a circle. Staple the ends together, linking it to the previous strip. Display the paper strips and explain that each link represents something one person can do to improve your school. Connecting the links demonstrates that this group of students has the power to make a lot of changes in the school's climate.

STEP 2—WARM FUZZY PROJECT

Distribute *Warm Fuzzy Forms* and pencils or pens. Explain that practicing cooperation to create *The Warm Fuzzy Project* will benefit the entire school. Students will be encouraged to write positive notes to friends, classmates, even teachers on blank *Warm Fuzzy Forms,* and each completed form will be delivered to the intended person. Members of this student group will be in charge of running the program.

Divide the group into teams to work on:

- Making posters
- Writing and delivering morning announcements
- Putting blank forms into teachers' mailboxes for distribution
- Collecting completed forms and delivering them to teachers' classrooms for distribution

ASSESSMENT—WARM FUZZY PROGRAM

The Warm Fuzzy Program may last as little as one week or as long as one month. After each team completes its assignments, members share the highlights and low points in a discussion, describing the parts that were the most fun or most rewarding and those that were hardest or most challenging.

INSPIRATIONAL QUOTE

As we let our light shine, we unconsciously give other people permission to do the same.

~ Marianne Williamson, activist

Warm Fuzzy Forms

SEND A WARM FUZZY TO SHOW YOU CARE!

My name is ____ .

My homeroom teacher's name is ______________________________ .

Please send a Warm Fuzzy to my friend ______________________________
(FIRST AND LAST NAME)

who is in Grade __________.

This person should get a Warm Fuzzy because ______________________________

____

____ .

SEND A WARM FUZZY TO SHOW YOU CARE!

My name is ____ .

My homeroom teacher's name is ______________________________ .

Please send a Warm Fuzzy to my classmate ______________________________
(FIRST AND LAST NAME)

who is in Grade __________.

This person should get a Warm Fuzzy because ______________________________

____

____ .

SEND A WARM FUZZY TO SHOW YOU CARE!

My name is ____ .

My homeroom teacher's name is ______________________________ .

Please send a Warm Fuzzy to my teacher ______________________________
(FIRST AND LAST NAME)

This person should get a Warm Fuzzy because ______________________________

____

____ .

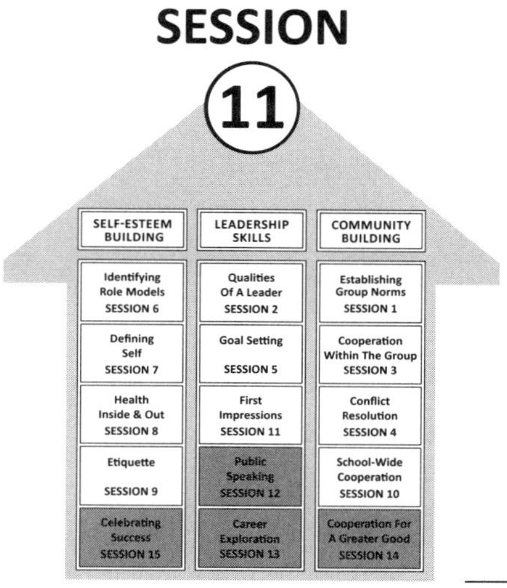

PILLAR 2
LEADERSHIP SKILLS

SKILL 3: FIRST IMPRESSIONS

Goal: Through participation in a group activity, students will gain awareness of the first impression their attire may make on others and learn about selecting appropriate clothing for different occasions.

MATERIALS NEEDED:

For the leader:

- ☐ Sticky notes
- ☐ Pen or marker
- ☐ 2-3 fashion magazines per student group
- ☐ Tagboard or medium-weight copy paper

For each student:

- ☐ 4 *Hanger Tags* (page 69)
- ☐ Scissors
- ☐ Pencil or pen
- ☐ Markers or colored pencils
- ☐ Program folder or binder

For each student group:

- ☐ Paper
- ☐ Pencil or pen

PRESENTATION:

STEP 1—ICEBREAKER

Distribute a pencil or pen and paper to each group. Begin with this icebreaker, which relates to first impressions:

> ***Impressions Of Me***: Organize students into groups of 5–10 members. Assign one person to be the recorder as each group discusses the following question:
>
> > *If someone looked at a picture of me today, what words would he or she use to describe the person in the picture?*

STEP 2—CLOTHING MESSAGES

Prior to the activity, label several sticky notes with *job interview, school, formal occasion.*

Three-member groups look through the magazines and find clothing to match each label. They may use the blank sticky notes to write their first impressions of clothing that might not fit into any of the named categories.

Each group presents the pictures of clothing they labeled and answers the following questions:

1. *Why did you give that outfit that label?*
2. *Why do you think that style sends that message?*
3. *How do you think a person would describe someone who wore that clothing in a very different setting?*

ASSESSMENT—HANGER TAGS

Distribute three to six tagboard/medium weight copies of *Hanger Tags* to each student and encourage the students to assess the clothing in their closets at home. They then complete the *Hanger Tags* by writing the appropriate place to wear each item, decorate and cut out the tags, and attach them to hangers for the identified outfits.

Practice Makes Perfect

(***Note:*** You may want to call in advance to talk with the store manager(s) and get permission.)

Take a field trip to a local clothing store and challenge students to work in teams to find appropriate clothing for different occasions.
OR
Organize a clothing scavenger hunt at your local mall. Divide students into teams and allow them to search at clothing stores for attire they would wear to different places. Provide disposable cameras so they can photograph their selections.

Hanger Tags

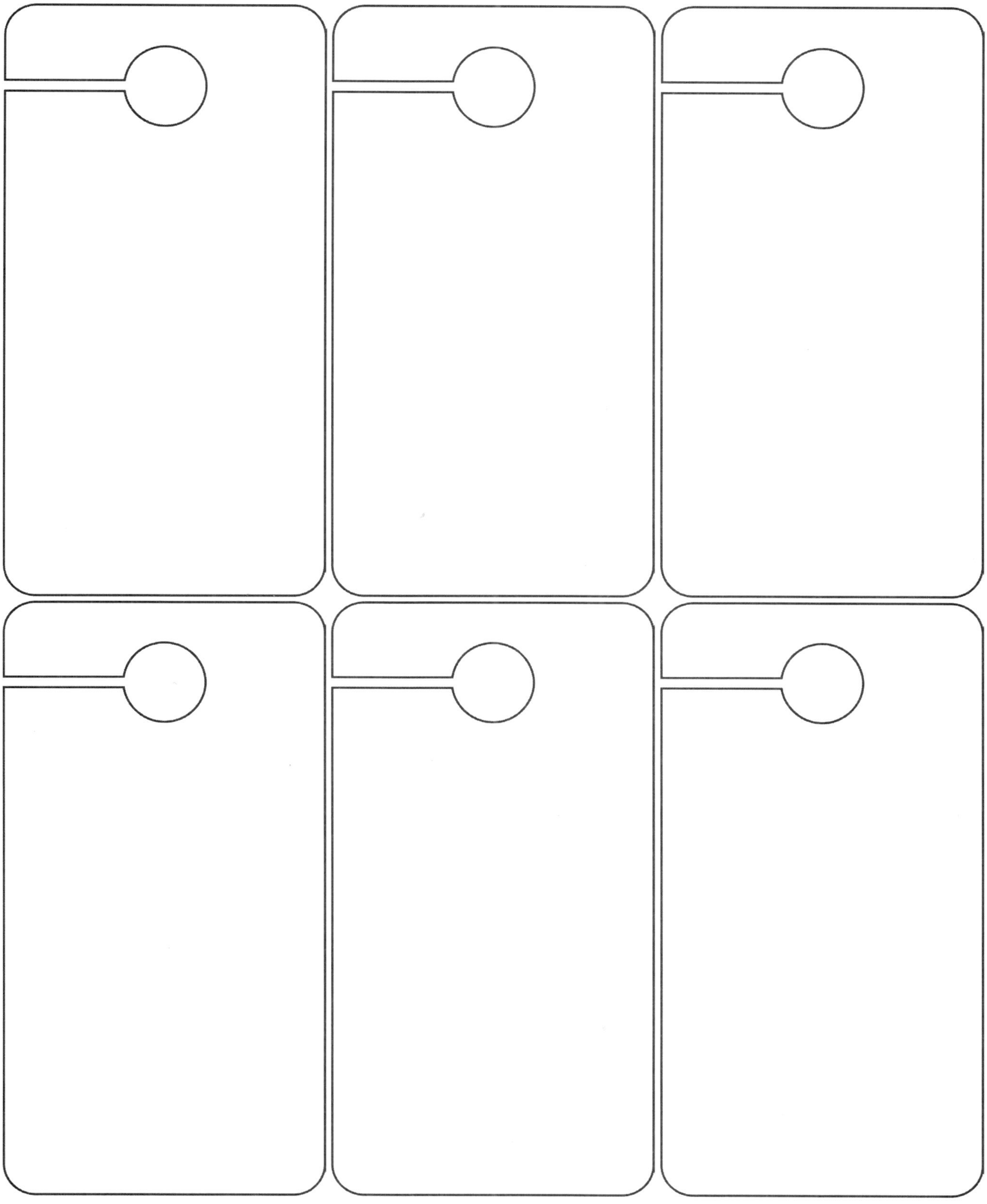

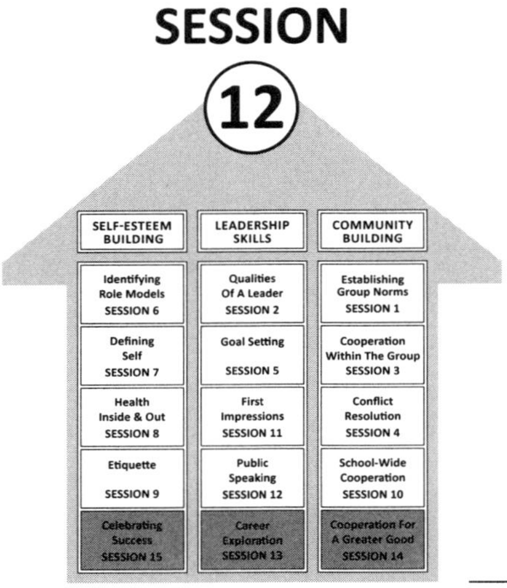

PILLAR 2
LEADERSHIP SKILLS

SKILL 4: PUBLIC SPEAKING

Goal: Listening to a guest presenter will teach students tips to make them more confident and more comfortable about public speaking.

MATERIALS NEEDED:

For the leader:

- ☐ Footage of a famous speech
- ☐ Invite a staff member, community or business leader, or parent to talk to the group about public speaking
- ☐ Video camera
- ☐ Podium or lectern (optional)

For each student:

- ☐ Completed assignments from previous sessions
- ☐ Program folder or binder

PRESENTATION:

STEP 1—ICEBREAKER

Begin with this icebreaker, which relates to public speaking:

> ***Speaking So People Will Listen***: After group members watch a short segment of a famous speech, lead a discussion of what made it a good speech. Ask: "What did the speaker do or say that made you want to listen or helped you remember what was said?"

STEP 2—GUEST SPEAKER

Ask the presenter to give tips on how to be an effective public speaker. Encourage him/her to share examples or stories to reinforce each tip.

At the end of the presentation, organize students into groups of 5–10 to discuss what tips they heard and why each one is important. Each group then reports back to the larger group.

ASSESSMENT—VIDEO PRACTICE

Inform group members that each of them will be videotaped giving a 5–10-minute speech. They may review assignments from previous lessons and select a topic. If possible, provide a podium or lectern and an audience.

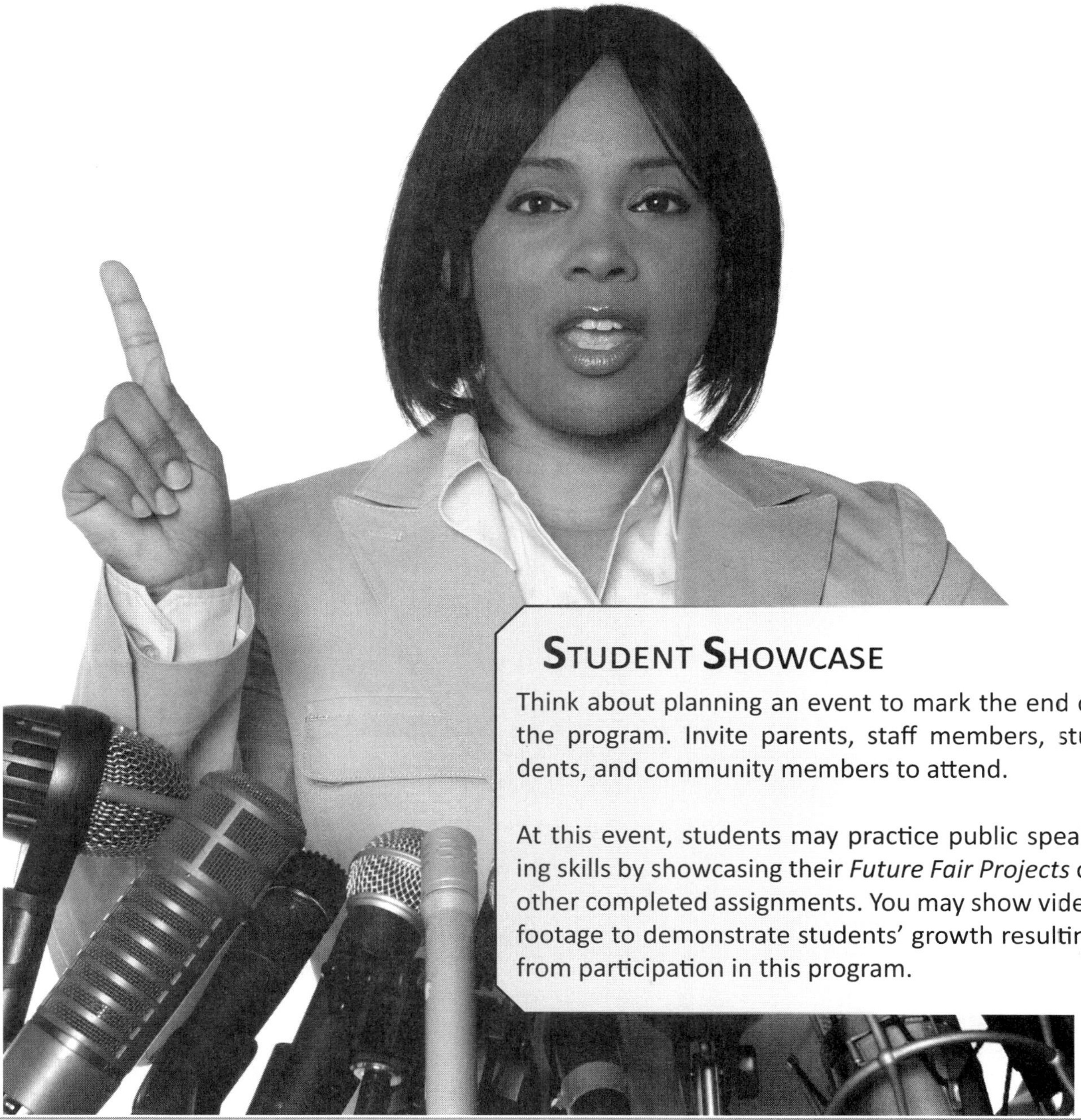

STUDENT SHOWCASE

Think about planning an event to mark the end of the program. Invite parents, staff members, students, and community members to attend.

At this event, students may practice public speaking skills by showcasing their *Future Fair Projects* or other completed assignments. You may show video footage to demonstrate students' growth resulting from participation in this program.

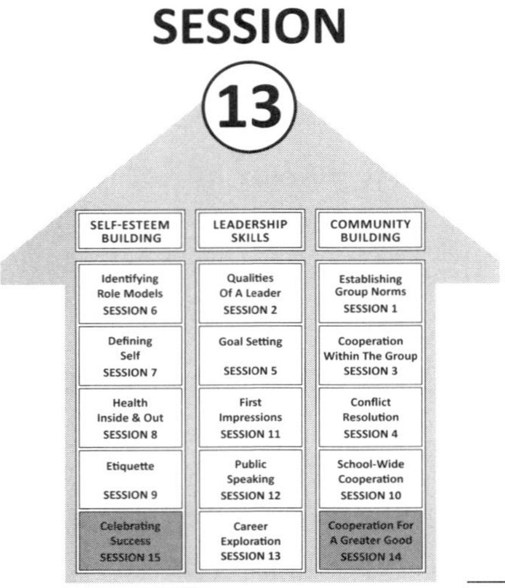

PILLAR 2
LEADERSHIP SKILLS

SKILL 5: CAREER EXPLORATION

Goal: By listening to guest speakers, students explore a variety of employment options to develop career goals.

MATERIALS NEEDED:

For the leader:

- ☐ *Career Lists* (pages 74-79)
- ☐ Tape
- ☐ Guest speakers

For each student:

- ☐ *Interests & Careers* (page 80)
- ☐ *Career Presenters–Exit Ticket* (page 81)
- ☐ Pencil or pen
- ☐ Program folder or binder

PRESENTATION:

STEP 1—ICEBREAKER

Begin with this icebreaker, which relates to careers:

> ***Career Corners***: Post *Career Lists* in various places throughout the room. Distribute *Interests & Careers* and pencils or pens. Allow the students move from list to list to complete the worksheet. Discuss which careers were of interest to them. (***Note***: The careers listed on pages 74-79 represent careers from the 16 Career Clusters.)

STEP 2—CAREER SPEAKERS

Invite parents and community members to be guest presenters. To give students the opportunity to hear about a variety of careers, be sure to include occupations from each of the *Career Lists.* Give special consideration to professions relating to math and science. Assign students to presenters of special interest to them or allow them to attend presentations of two speakers they choose.

ASSESSMENT—CAREER SPEAKERS EXIT TICKET:

Prior to the presentations, distribute *Career Presenters–Exit Tickets*. Students write new information they learned, additional questions they have for the speaker, or notes on each presentation.

Students may place completed assignments in their program folder or take the assignments home.

ON-THE-JOB TRAINING

Arrange a tour of a local business. Inquire about having women who work there talk during the tour about their particular responsibilities.

Find women willing to mentor students by letter or e-mail. Have each group member write an introductory letter with five questions she would like to ask.

CAREER LIST

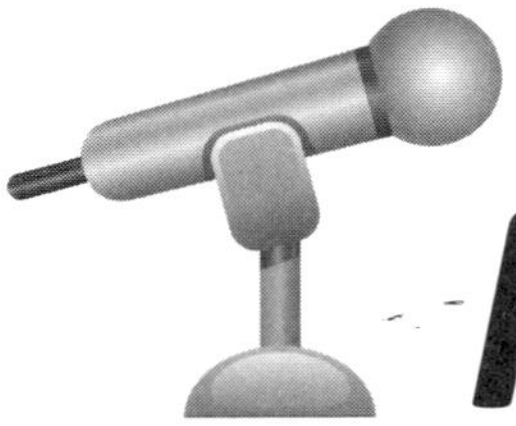

Music & Art

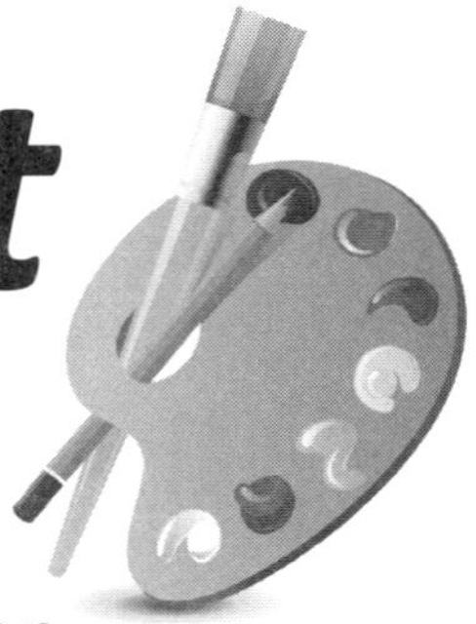

- Band/Orchestra Musician
- Booking Agent
- Instrument Repairer
- Instrument Tuner
- Music Teacher
- Songwriter
- Dancer
- Actor
- Dance Instructor
- Ice Skater
- Photographer
- Designer
- Illustrator
- Painter
- Photo Editor
- Sculptor
- Archivist & Curator
- Botanist
- Historian
- Librarian
- Painting Restorer
- Records Manager
- Musician
- Cartoonist
- Animator
- Architect
- Commercial Artist
- Fashion Artist
- Graphic Designer
- Illustrator
- Web Page Designer
- Multi-Media Artist
- Chef
- Disc Jockey
- News Reporter
- Public Relations Specialist
- Sales Worker
- Television Announcer

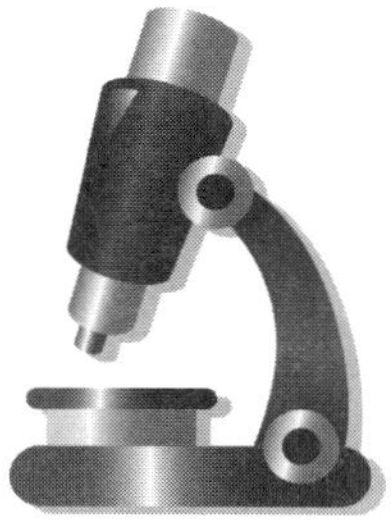

CAREER LIST

Science

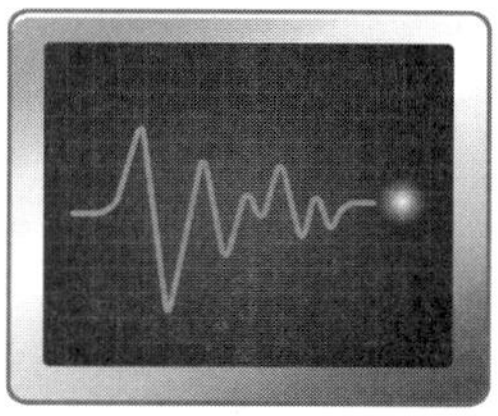

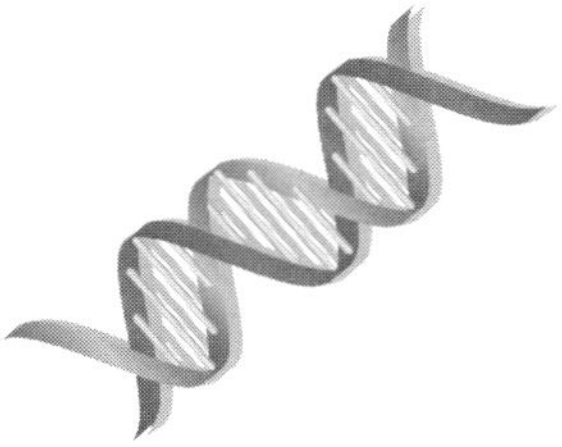

Pharmacist

Biologist

Chemist

Medical Scientist

Pharmacy Technician

Videogame Designer

Food Scientist

Physicist

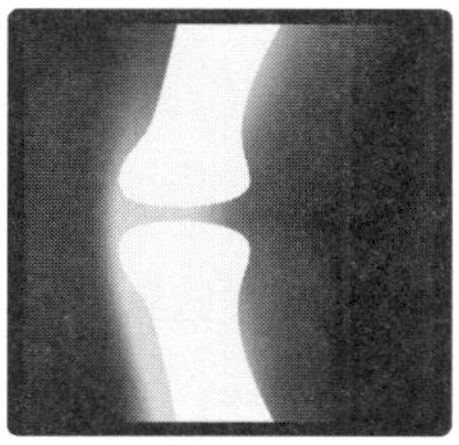

Doctor

Acupuncturist

Audiologist

Chiropractor

Dentist

Nurse Practitioner

Optometrist

Podiatrist

Speech Pathologist

Veterinarian

Nurse

Emergency Medical Technician

Occupational Therapist

Physical Therapist

Physician Assistant

Pilot

Air-Traffic Controller

Computer Repairer

Appliance Repairer

Automotive Electrician

Broadcast & Sound Technician

Electronic Home Entertainment Equipment Repairer

Power-Tool Repairer

Telephone Repairer

Web Developer

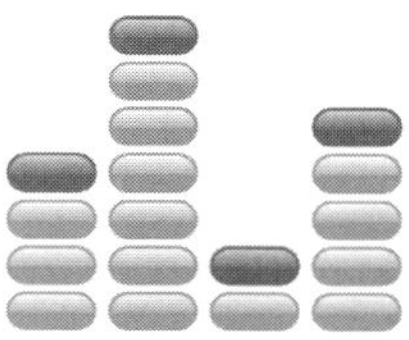

CAREER LIST

Gym & Outdoors

Professional Athlete

Coach

Trainer

Recreational Therapist

Umpire/Referee

Aerobics Instructor

Fitness Trainer

Occupational Therapist

Personal Trainer

Physical Therapist

Carpenter

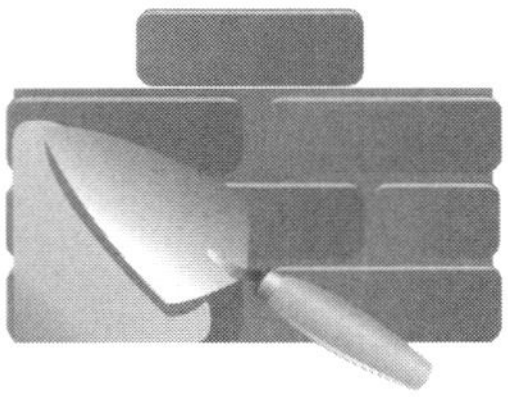

Bricklayer

Plumber

Stonemason

Surveyor

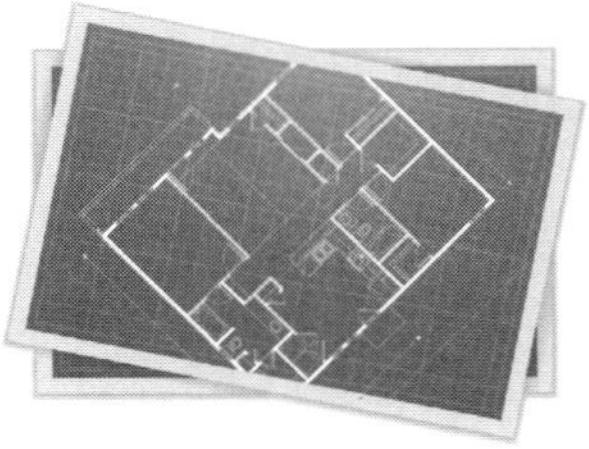

Architect

Civil Engineer

Landscape Architect

Urban Planner

Veterinarian

Zookeeper

Livestock Farm Worker

Rancher

Retail Sales Pet Store Worker

Wildlife Biologist

Zoologist

CAREER LIST

Social Studies

- Lawyer
- FBI Special Agent
- Journalist
- Judge
- Law Clerk

- Correctional Officer
- Guard
- Police Officer
- Private Detective

- Inspector
- Fire Marshal
- Politician

- Corporate Chief Executive
- Military Officer
- Car Salesperson
- Insurance Agent
- Retail Salesperson
- Landscape Architect
- Travel Agent
- Urban Planner

- City Manager
- Civil Engineer
- Real Estate Agent
- Architect
- Clergy

- Counselor
- Social Worker
- Teacher
- Event Planner

- Personal Shopping Assistant

CAREER LIST

Language Arts

Reporter

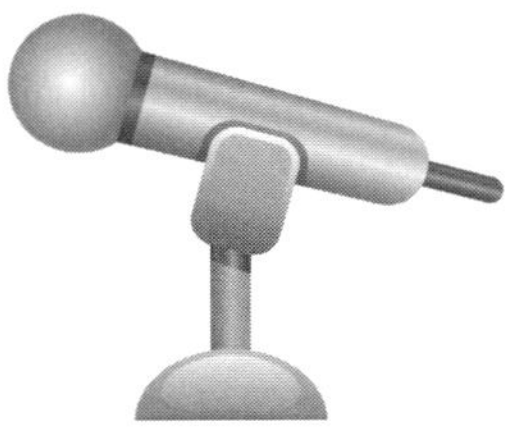

Announcer

Editor

Interpreter

Teacher

College/University Professor

Counselor

Education Administrator

Social Worker

Special Education Teacher

Trainer

Librarian

Museum Curator

Records Manager

Secretary

Bookkeeper

Court Reporter

Receptionist

Medical Assistant

Medical Record Technician

Office Manager

Writer

Advertising Writer or Designer

Newspaper Reporter

CAREER LIST

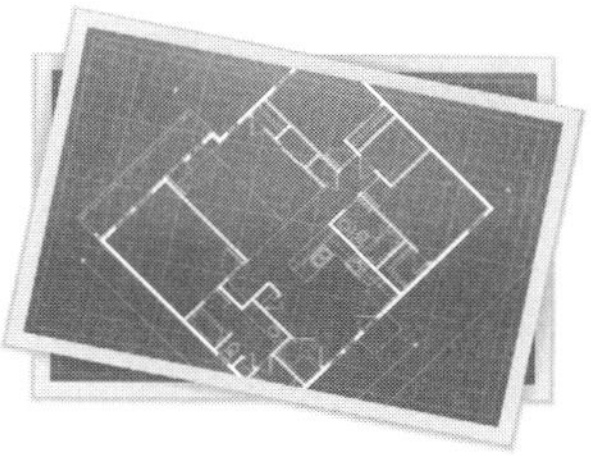

Math

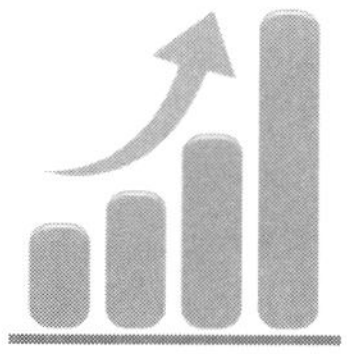

- Engineer
- Architect
- Mathematician
- Physical Scientist
- Accountant
- Bank Officer
- FBI Special Agent
- Financial Analyst
- Loan Officer
- Personal Financial Advisor
- Tax Collector/Revenue Agent
- Cashier
- Teller
- Clerk
- Food & Beverage Server

- Post Office Worker
- Architect
- Construction Manager
- Interior Designer
- Graphic Designer
- Landscape Architect
- Urban Planner
- Computer Hardware Engineer
- Computer Programmer
- Computer Software Engineer
- Mechanic
- Computer Repairer
- Heating, Air-Conditioning, & Refrigeration Mechanic
- Home Appliance Repairer
- Industrial Machinery Repairer

Interests & Careers

There is a whole world of work,

and you can learn about jobs that relate to things you like to do.

Below, write down some things that you like to do inside and outside school. Find careers that relate to those interests.

My favorite subjects in school are:

1. ______________________________

2. ______________________________

3. ______________________________

→

Some of my favorite things to do when I'm not in school are:

1. ______________________________

2. ______________________________

3. ______________________________

→

Here are some careers that relate to my interests (find at least one for each):

Other Careers That Interested Me

In the space below, write any other careers that you heard about today that sound interesting to you.

Career Presenters—Exit Ticket

Presenter's Name ______________________________

List three things you learned during this session:

____

____

____

Notes:

____

____

____

Presenter's Name ______________________________

List three things you learned during this session:

____

____

____

Notes:

____

____

____

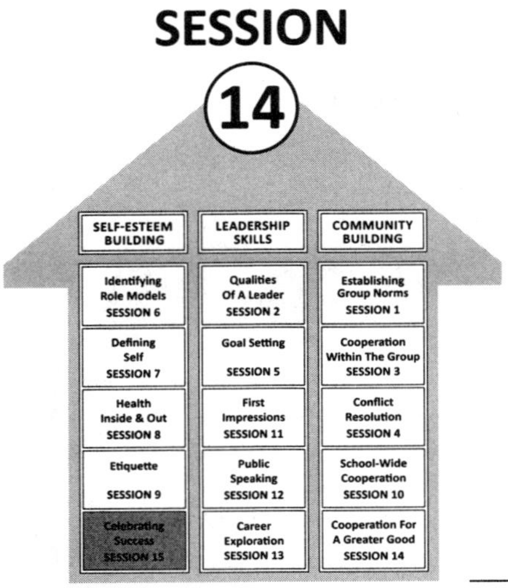

PILLAR 3
COMMUNITY BUILDING

SKILL 5: COOPERATION FOR A GREATER GOOD

Goal: Students and coordinators participate in group discussion to create a unifying, goal-directed community-service project.

MATERIALS NEEDED:

For the leader:

- ☐ None

For each student group:

- ☐ Paper
- ☐ Pencil or pen

PRESENTATION:

STEP 1—ICEBREAKER

Begin with this icebreaker, which relates to community service.

Community Service–What, Why, and Who: Begin with a discussion of community service. Ask the following questions and discuss students' responses:

1. *What is* community service?
2. *Why is community service important?*
3. *What groups in our community are in need of support?*

STEP 2—PROJECT PLANNING

Organize students into groups of 10 to brainstorm community-service ideas. Each group shares its ideas with the larger group and the group as a whole selects a project that meets the following criteria:

Project Ideas

Homeless Shelter
Baby-Supply Drive
Holiday Season Non-Perishable Food Collection
Winter Coat Drive
School Supply Drive

1. Will it help people in our community?
2. Is it something we can organize ourselves?
3. Do we have the supplies and resources to make this happen?

STEP 3—PROJECT COMPLETION

After students select a project, lead a discussion of the next steps. Give paper and a pen or pencil to each group's appointed recorder. Help students divide into action groups, carry out each step in their project plan, and make decisions about:

1. How long the project will last
2. Whether to use flyers, posters, morning announcements, or other methods to advertise their project to the school
3. How each group member will help complete the project

Until the community service project has been completed, allow 15 minutes at the end of each meeting to discuss the project and work on it. You may wish to schedule additional meetings to allow students time to complete necessary tasks and discuss their feelings about working on a community-service initiative.

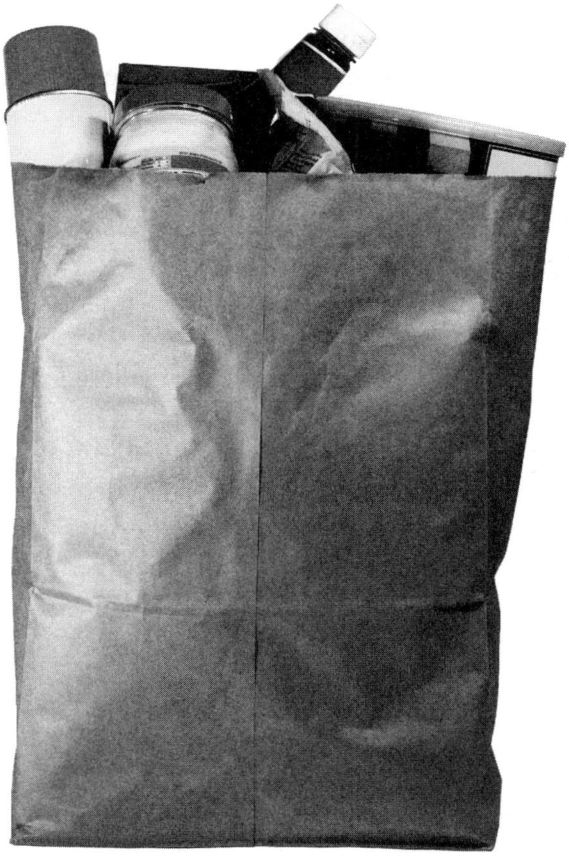

ASSESSMENT—HIGH-LOW DISCUSSIONS

Throughout the project, students share highlights and low points of this assignment, discussing the most rewarding and most challenging aspects.

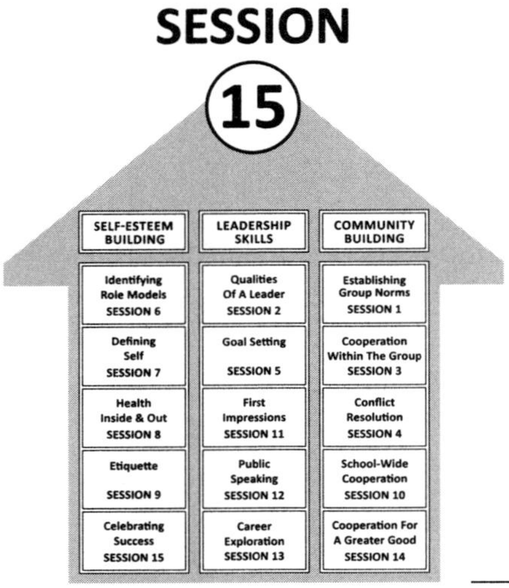

PILLAR 1
SELF-ESTEEM BUILDING

SKILL 5: CELEBRATING SUCCESS

Goal: Awards presentations will recognize group members' achievements and reinforce student improvements.

MATERIALS NEEDED:

For the leader:

- ☐ None

For each student:

- ☐ Poster board or large piece of paper
- ☐ Marker and other art supplies
- ☐ *Shining Star* (page 86)
- ☐ Pencil or pen
- ☐ Scissors
- ☐ *A Letter To Myself* written in Session 1

PRESENTATION:

STEP 1— ICEBREAKER

Begin with this icebreaker, centered around celebrating group members' successes:

> ***Praise Board***: Each student prints her name in large letters at the top of the piece of poster board or paper board leaving a blank space in the center, then decorates her poster. Students display their posters around the room, then write words of praise, thanks, or congratulations on other members' posters.

STEP 2—SHINING STAR AWARDS

Distribute *Shining Star* and pencils or pens. Each group member thinks of an academic achievement, a behavioral goal, or a personal change she accomplished this year. She writes her name on the banner of her *Shining Star* and her success story inside the star, then cuts out the star. Discuss the importance of celebrating personal successes and making new plans once a goal has been reached.

CONCLUDING THE PROGRAM

To help students find closure, review completed program folders as a group. Consider taking time at the conclusion of this meeting to allow students to independently read the *Letter To Myself* written during the initial meeting. Encourage participants to look back on the progress made during the year as reflected in the letter and completed activities.

PARENT INVOLVEMENT

This program includes many opportunities for parent involvement as presenters, field trip chaperones, or new-skill practice partners. Think about inviting all parents to attend the last session. Students can make their *Shining Stars* in advance and hang them from the ceiling for parents to admire.

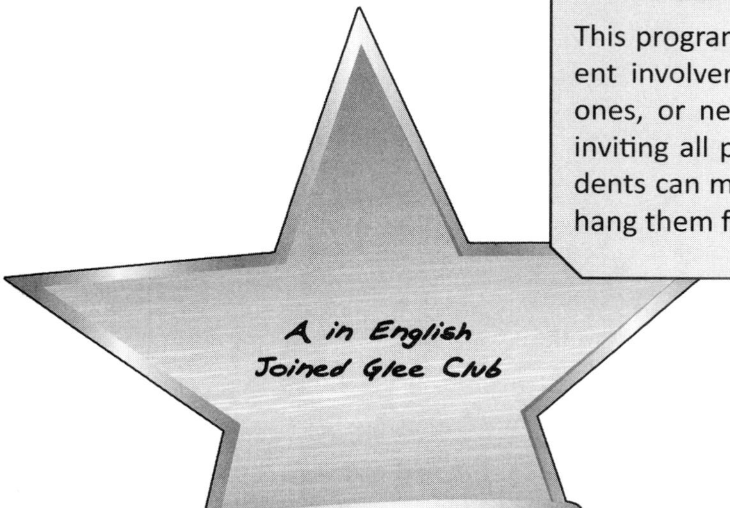

SHINING STAR

References

1 Dinkes R, Kemp J and Baum K. *Indicators of school crime and safety: 2008* (NCES 2009–022/NCJ 226343). Washington, DC: U.S. Department of Education, Institute of Education Sciences, National Center for Education Statistics, and U.S. Department of Justice, Office of Justice Programs, Bureau of Justice Statistics, 2009.

2 Boccanfuso C and Kuhfeld M. Multiple responses, promising results: Evidence-based nonpunative alternatives to zero tolerance. *Research-to-Results*, March 2011. Available at: http://www.childtrends.org/Files/Child_Trends-2011_03_01_RB_AltToZeroTolerance.pdf. Accessed March 14, 2012.

3 Durlak JA and Weissberg R P *The impact of after-school programs that promote personal and social skills.* Chicago, IL: Collaborative for Academic, Social, and Emotional Learning, 2007.

4 Payton, J, Weissberg RP, Durlak JA, Dymnicki AB, Taylor RD Schellinger KB, et al. The positive impact of social and emotional learning for kindergarten to eighth-grade students: Findings from three scientific reviews. Chicago, IL: Collaborative for Academic, Social, and Emotional Learning, 2008.

5 Social and Character Development Research Consortium. *Efficacy of schoolwide programs to promote social and character development and reduce problem behavior in elementary school children.* Washington, DC: National Center for Education Research, Institute of Education Sciences, U.S. Department of Education, 2010.

About The Author

Melanie Martin is a certified professional school counselor who has worked at the elementary and secondary levels in Baltimore County Public Schools. As a presenter, she has provided professional development to school counselors throughout Maryland on such topics as technology integration, learning and leadership styles, and creating impactful groups for girls. Melanie has served as president of the Baltimore County Association for Counseling and Development and newsletter editor for the Maryland School Counselor Association. As a program coordinator for United Way of Central Maryland, she worked to organize and oversee a girls mentoring program for Cover Girl Cosmetics/Procter & Gamble. Melanie and her husband Phillip are the proud parents of a daughter Nysa and a son Isaiah.